FAILURE
TO
SCREAM

FAILURE TO SCREAM

ROBERT HICKS

THOMAS NELSON PUBLISHERS

Nashville

Published in Nashville, Tennessee, by Oliver-Nelson Books, a division of Thomas Nelson, Inc., Publishers, and distributed in Canada by Lawson Falle, Ltd., Cambridge, Ontario.

Circle of Assumptions is from the book *Returning Home* by Robert M. Hicks, copyright © 1991 by Robert Hicks. Used by permission of Baker Book House.

Stages of Recovery from Traumatic Events is from Charles R. Figley's "From Victim to Survivor" in *Trauma and Its Wake* (New York: Brunner, Mazel, 1985) and is reprinted with permission.

The Bible version used in this publication is THE NEW KING JAMES VERSION. Copyright © 1979, 1980, 1982, Thomas Nelson, Inc., Publishers.

Printed in the United States of America.

Library of Congress Cataloging-in-Publication Data

Hicks, Robert, 1945–
    Failure to scream / Robert Hicks.
       p.   cm.
    Includes bibliographical references.
    ISBN 0-8407-9127-5 (hard)
    1. Post-traumatic stress disorder—Patients—Religious life. 2. Post-traumatic stress disorder—Religious aspects—Christianity. 3. Post-traumatic stress disorder—Case studies. I. Title.
BV4910.45.H53   1993
616.85'210651—dc20   92-33394
                                     CIP

1 2 3 4 5 6 — 98 97 96 95 94 93

To
the family members of the 137 killed
on Delta flight 191, August 2, 1985,
at Dallas-Fort Worth Airport.
Their scream is not over.

To
those who survived the crash
and are still screaming.

To
the Delta marketing representatives,
Red Cross volunteers, and military personnel
who created and staffed our caring cocoon
at the Dallas-Fort Worth Hilton. We have our own unique
bonds of pain and continue to scream.

CONTENTS

ACKNOWLEDGMENTS

In some ways I consider my early childhood and adolescence fairly routine and untraumatic. Compared to what I see in counseling today, my childhood was sheltered and problem-free. Therefore, I owe my education to the subjects presented in this book to many who have played very important roles in showing me what the other side of life is like.

First of all, I thank the families of the victims of the Delta 191 crash, who taught me so much about what it means to scream and rage at life's most unfair events. In many ways, this book began with them. The pain they shared, the surprising humor displayed in the midst of absurdity, and the raw courage I saw are all noted in this book. I also acknowledge Mike and Marilyn Steinberg, a vibrant couple who walked away from the crash with only minor scratches and burns. They were instrumental in the healing of other family members by their openness and willingness to help others who needed more understanding. To our caring cocoon established in the Hilton Hotel, I give Dr. James Black, Father Brown, and Silvia LaRue a hearty thank you. Each of you and many others whose names I can't remember contributed greatly to my own understanding and healing.

I also want to mention the valuable contribution of the Society for Traumatic-Stress Studies. The society has functioned as both a clearinghouse for research and a place where those of us who have gone through similar traumatic experiences can process them with others who understand. Thanks go to Dr. Charles Figley for having the vision of starting such an organization to address the unique aspects of traumatic stress in the lay and professional communities.

Learning is always interactional; therefore, it is sometimes difficult to separate one's own ideas from those of others. Several key players in my life on the subject of trauma have been my fellow team members in the Critical-Incident Stress course taught at the Maxwell Air Force Base Chaplains' School. In particular, I have appreciated the joint perspective this course has displayed in bringing together the insights from medicine, psychology, and theology in the lives of very esteemed professionals. Maj. (Dr.) Harry Howitt, Lt. Col. (Dr.) Bill Kelleher, and Dr. Carol Fullerton earn much credit for stimulating my thinking and contributing greatly to the research base for this book. The chapter on what we have learned from the walking wounded could not have been written without their current and solidly based research and professional opinion.

Col. Robert Maloney (U.S. Air Force, retired) has provided much insight and information about the mortuary-services procedures at Dover Air Force Base, Delaware. I have greatly appreciated the briefings he has given at the Maxwell Air Force Base Chaplains' School, meetings of the Society for Traumatic-Stress Studies, and the surgeon general's conference. Little does he know how much he has expanded and enhanced the role of the chaplain in traumatic-stress studies. By sharing his perspectives on the chaplain's involvement with him after the Gander Army Airborne crash, the Lebanon Marine Corps barracks fiasco, the space-shuttle disaster, and others, he has greatly enhanced the critical role of the chaplain during these traumatic events.

I would also like to thank my fellow Air National Guard chaplain, 1st Lt. Greg Clapper (Iowa), for making available his thorough and detailed after-action report from the United Airlines crash in Sioux City. It has provided much "real life-and-death" information other professionals and care-givers need to prepare themselves for such events.

Credit must also be given to those who have entered my life through traditional counseling, ongoing community accidents, and the normal traumas that enter one's life merely by getting older. All such experiences noted in this book are actual, reflecting the true nature of what was faced by those suffering the tragedies. However, in most cases names and locations have been changed to respect the privacy of the persons' identities.

I thank my publisher, Victor Oliver, for responding to the idea of doing a book on this subject. I so appreciate working with a publisher who sees the need and relevance of addressing the tough, human-dilemma questions.

Words cannot express the difficulty of writing a book in the midst of doing so many other things. Trying to stay on top of my teaching responsibilities, family commitments, and military involvement while writing a book is no easy task. It takes an employer and a family who at least share a vision for the book-writing process. I thank the faculty and administration of the Seminary of the East for their understanding, encouragement, and valuable input.

Finally, I wish to express to my family how greatly I value their encouragement and love. They are my deepest source of inspiration and by far my best sales staff! Thanks also go to my mother-in-law, Ann Rosenburg, for providing her "High Places" mountain home, where this book could be conceived and finally brought to completion. Overlooking the beautiful Appalachian and Blue Ridge Mountains just outside Blowing Rock, North Carolina, it provided the perfect locale to stimulate thought and cure writer's block.

Robert Hicks
Christmas Day, 1991

FAILURE
TO
SCREAM

I wanted to scream but I had no mouth.
Ray Bradbury

INTRODUCTION

This is a book about screaming—or, more precisely, the failure to scream. When we are hurt, are injured, are molested, suffer abuse, face a debilitating illness, or get fired, we feel the need to express our pain. The process of expressing and dealing with pain, of letting the pain out, is a scream of sorts. This scream is not necessarily the intense emotional expression of a loud yell or noise usually associated with the word *scream*. Some people, in fact, may do their screaming through emotional outbursts that clearly reveal how badly they have been hurt. Others may stuff the pain inside and deny its existence by minimizing the effects and going on with their lives as usual. This avoidance of pain and hurt for whatever reasons is what I call throughout this book the failure to scream. It is a denial of feelings and processes necessary to find meaning in the traumatic experience. Burying one's pain is unhealthy. The individual outwardly may continue to appear well but inwardly may never grow beyond the moment of the traumatic event. The result is being emotionally trapped in time, waiting for a psychic explosion that will eventually happen. For some, this expression of pain may be like a slow leak. For others it may be a more dramatic snap, when all feelings come out at once. But what has produced both is the same, the failure to process grief.

The scream I'm talking about is not necessarily the intense emotional verbalization of some primal-scream therapy. Extroverts may do their screaming in overt ways, letting everyone know how badly they have been hurt through actual yelling and screaming. But for most, the scream I am talking about in this book is the very deep-seated psychic scream that is not allowed to emerge. This scream will be described later in technical terms, but for now I will call it the emotional inner rage that arises in response to traumatic events. For the most part, the scream is kept under the surface and is seen only in glimpses when certain things in the environment trigger a more overt reaction. In this sense, the scream may never be apparent to others; they can't even see it. Many victims will not allow themselves the freedom to scream and give proper venting to this normal reaction. They may never talk about it or want to talk about it, even when asked to do so. Thus, they fail to give expression to this inner hidden scream.

This failure to scream is what the book is about. It is about people who have been through the worst disasters, tragedies, and inhuman experiences. But for whatever reasons they do not give vent to their screams at the time. Therefore, their screaming is delayed, put off until a later date, and often disguised by coping mechanisms that appear "normal." However, we as humans were made to scream, and scream we will. If we fail to scream in response to the pain we feel, we only prolong the screaming or divert it in other directions. The following true accounts reveal what this failure to scream is all about.

On August 2, 1985, an L1011 jumbo jet on its approach to the Dallas-Fort Worth Airport descended through extreme turbulence, hit a wind shear, and dropped half a mile in altitude. The Delta jet touched down in pastureland about a mile short of the runway, tried to get back into the air, then hit a passing car just north of the airport. The plane sliced off the top of the car and decapitated the driver. The innocent passerby in the vehicle was the first of many killed in the fire and rain that followed. After hitting the car, the Delta jumbo veered left off the runway and continued on a direct collision course with a set of steel water tanks just southeast of the airport. The plane exploded on impact, severing the tail section from the aircraft, which slid down the tarmac. All who survived were those in the rear section of the aircraft.

I remember watching the news coverage that evening, which appeared on every Dallas station. An on-the-scene reporter thrust a microphone into the face of Anthony Rogers and asked him about what he had seen. Rogers had been driving the car following the one hit by the plane. In the blinding rainstorm he had pulled off route 114 and had run to the demolished car ahead of him to see if he could help. There was nothing he could do. Later, with news cameras rolling, he unemotionally detailed what he had seen. I was impressed that a man who saw such things could be so calm, so objective, and so unaffected by the horror he had just witnessed. It was as if he were calmly describing what happened at work that particular day. I even turned to my wife and commented how emotionally "together" he seemed . . . too together!

Nine months later, while glancing through a Dallas newspaper, I came across the following headline: "Police Seek Man Missing in Irving."[1] The entire article focused on the resultant problems this young man had experienced since the crash. The article detailed that he had disappeared and that the local police were trying to find him. His roommate said, "Rogers was an excellent student, with a 3.5 grade point average, but he dropped out of school after the crash. He just couldn't study for seeing that guy there."[2] One day he left to go on some errands and never returned. His moment in the limelight of the camera had not presented what was really going on inside the inner, remote areas of his personhood. On the outside he was composed, articulate, objective. Inside he was screaming. But we didn't see the screaming. Neither did he. His screaming came later. He had failed to scream at the time.

Martha was having sexual problems in her marriage. She desperately wanted to give herself to her husband, yet something was always there, holding her back. When they made love, she always felt used or numb. When asked how long this particular problem had been going on, she replied, "It's gotten worse ever since my father became ill." As I pursued any connection between her declining father's health and the problems in her marriage, she finally blurted out, "I think I was sexually abused by my father." I responded, "What do you mean, 'You *think* you were abused'? Either you were or you weren't." She went on to express how her father had once put her to bed when she was a teenager and had begun caressing her breasts. It was only once. It never happened again, and they never talked about it afterward. But now that her father was in ailing health, her recollection of the event was coming back. The thoughts of the experience were carrying over into her sexual relationship with her husband. Was there a connection? When asked how she felt about the experience when it happened, she responded, "I don't know. It never happened again, so I guess I never thought about it much." I added, "How do you think someone *should* feel about such an experience?" She answered, "I don't know." She really didn't know. She loved her father, but at the same time, she had a deep-seated distrust of him that carried over to all men, including her husband.

What is the appropriate feeling for being abused, even the way Martha was? The range of feelings runs from the fundamental loss of innocence and trust, to rage, to an all-consuming bitterness toward the world. What is normal when wronged and abused by one who supposedly loves you is a significant sense of loss. When we suffer loss, we should scream. But Martha hadn't screamed. She didn't know what to do with her loss of innocence. So she buried it. She had failed to scream, so her screaming would have to come later.

Corporal Smith was known in his unit as a gung ho tough guy. One had to be tough to go behind the lines and plant the concealed sensors that monitored the Vietcong supply lines and troop movements. To put them in was one thing; to go back and get them out was another. One never knew what he might find either going in or coming back. Life was lived on the edge. The edge produced a certain high, an adrenaline rush, that would never be matched by the rest of civilian life. Corporal Smith had knifed Vietcongs. He had seen buddies blown away and others seriously wounded by hidden Claymore mines.

Twenty years later, Corporal Smith, with three kids and a wife, can't understand how he could have done many of the things he did as a young nineteen-year-old corporal. He once asked me how I could explain the sheer pleasure of the violence he had done. Now these memory tapes play back in his mind, and they are abhorrent to him; but at the same time, he can still feel the rush, the pleasure, the personal sense of satisfaction that came from the killing fields. "In 'nam it didn't mean nothin'." Now twenty years later, it does. The gung ho Corporal Smith is a middle-aged businessman who is starting to scream. The pain of Vietnam is surfacing. His screaming is silent, safely concealed in his head, but it is screaming just the same. He failed to scream twenty years ago, so he screams now.

Ginny is a mother of three—or should I say two? What does one say after a child has died? She *was* the mother of three, she still sees herself as the mother of three, but she is now the mother of two. Her ten-year-old daughter was killed in a freak swimming accident in her own backyard. One minute she was swimming, laughing with her friends, and the next she was submerged facedown at the deep end of the pool. Friends didn't see what had happened, heard nothing. But for all close to the event, the reality was the same: an unbelievably tragic event had happened.

For Ginny the memory is still present almost daily. She has survived but not well. Ginny came in for counseling when her husband was laid off from work. In counseling she became more aware of the building effect of her many painful experiences. The first was being a child of an alcoholic father and later a child of divorce. When asked how she felt about her parents' divorce, she uttered, "How *I* felt? I don't remember anyone ever asking me how I felt. One day our dad was there; the next he was gone. But I was only twelve at the time, so I don't remember much." Kids are often not allowed to scream emotionally, or they may not know enough about what is happening to scream emotionally, or perhaps they don't think adults will like them if they scream. That was Ginny. She was screaming in her late thirties. Some of the screaming was delayed. The death of her daughter and then the loss of her husband's work had only exaggerated the scream. Now the screaming was multiple, massive, and immobilizing.

As I write this introduction, the evening news is reporting another mass murder. This time it is in Kileen, Texas, where George Hennard, a disturbed loner, crashed his truck into Luby's Cafeteria and then opened up on the noon diners with two semiautomatic weapons. Twenty-two died, with another twenty being injured. It goes down as the worst mass shooting in U.S. history.[3] For each one in the cafeteria there will be much screaming to be done in the future. One does not walk away from such an event and go home without having some sleepless nights or recurring intrusions of the event into the mind. Many will try to forget it as soon as possible or pretend that it didn't affect them. Their failure to scream will cause other problems and put off their screaming to a later date.

What each of these experiences illustrates is a common phenomenon. That phenomenon is a delayed-response mechanism built into every human being. When someone hits us, or when our finger is cut, we feel pain. The pain is a gift. The pain sends us a message, a message that something is not right. The pain produces a response. We shout, "Ouch!" or worse vulgarities, we cry, we get angry, we withdraw to bandage our wounds and buy healing time. What is abnormal is to feel nothing when hit, cut, or hurt. Physical pain produces immediate physical and emotional responses that are normal and natural to human beings. An individual through discipline and denial may be able to put his hand over a burning flame (like G. Gordon Liddy in his book *Will*), but he will still have his hand burned, and a burned hand will be painful. When this happens, screaming or the need to scream follows.

The same is true of emotional pain. If we don't take the time to scream when painful events hit us, we will do our screaming later. But we all scream. We were made to scream. The scream is a gift, a reminder that we are what we are . . . human beings who have feelings. We are not robots or computers who can take punishment and, apart from having our programs scrambled, feel nothing. It is human to feel. It is inhuman not to feel. It is human to scream. It is inhuman not to scream. When we don't scream in response to the pain we feel, we only delay the scream. This failure to scream prolongs and often complicates the scream at a later date.

The delayed response to emotional pain as seen in each of the preceding illustrations is what this book attempts to detail. In clinical jargon it has a specific term (posttraumatic-stress disorder or PTSD), but for the purposes of this book I call it the failure to scream. Once thought of as a problem only among Vietnam veterans, it is now commonly recognized as one of the most basic responses to any kind of trauma, no matter how severe or minor. The failure-to-scream dynamic is seen in abuse victims, children of divorce, dysfunctional families, alcoholics, Holocaust survivors, those involved in natural disasters, and anyone who works around traumatic events (fire fighters, police officers, medical personnel, and clergy). Even unemployment, work crisis, and family problems sometimes produce the same symptoms. Loss of loved ones or being close to the loss of life personally is very traumatic. Some see raising teenagers or the mid-life crisis as a sort of traumatic event that can produce the same tendency to deny the scream. The current AIDS epidemic is shattering the lives of thousands, perhaps even millions. Accompanying each diagnosis of HIV-positive, an entire family and set of friends enter a grief process. For most of these the acknowledgment puts them into severe traumatic stress. Some scream; some don't. Much of the screaming comes later. Even retirement and adjusting to old age, with its accompanying health declines, can be traumatic. In each situation our psychic response is one of screaming, but for various reasons we don't. Whether we are trying to be tough, not wanting to be perceived a certain way, or just not taking the time, we don't scream. The failure to scream causes long-term problems for ourselves and others.

If you have failed to scream in some areas of your life, then this book is for you. If you are encountering certain unexplainable responses within yourself that seem to be rooted in a sense of loss, then this book may help you understand those feelings. If you have a loved one or a friend who is doing a lot of screaming now that you don't understand, this book may help you understand what she is going through. You may want to turn quickly to chapter 2 and read the description of what a traumatized person looks like. More often than not, if you have picked up the book or have already purchased it, you are dealing with something or someone who is already screaming or needs to scream.

The road I am attempting to travel in this book is to share some personal and professional insights into this thing called posttraumatic-stress disorder. I do not consider myself an expert in the field, but I have worked in the field specifically for the past ten years. I have had my own traumas to work through, and I am still working through others. In professional capacities I have been involved in several major traumatic events and have worked with other professionals in the field. As a military chaplain I have worked with veterans from Vietnam to Desert Storm. In 1985 I was placed on active duty by the Texas Air National Guard to coordinate the care of families after the Delta 191 crash at the Dallas-Fort Worth Airport. The crash claimed 137 lives out of 152 passengers. In the aftermath I gave death notifications to families and worked with several of the survivors. As a counselor I have had my share of traumatic events in the lives of others: brain-dead children on life support, car accidents that killed close friends, sexual abuse of women and children, friends charged with crimes, HIV-positive clients, and too many divorces and family problems to mention. In many ways, after a few years the accumulated traumas of others begin to make even the therapist traumatized vicariously. I have been in the house of trauma and might still live there from time to time. The insights I share are mine, but their genesis is not always original with me. I have tried to give credit along the way to those who have helped shape my thought and who have provided some helpful handles by which to understand some complex human functioning. Avail yourself of the credits at the beginning of the book for their unique contributions. They have taught me how to recognize the scream and to understand better the screaming of others.

We had better learn about screaming because *trauma* may be the watchword of the future. In one of our after-action meetings following the Delta crash, Mike Reilly, then director of disaster services for the American Red Cross, said, "Trauma is the vision of the future. . . . From our aging airliner fleets to the decaying of our eastern cities' infrastructures (water and sanitation systems), which are too costly and largely impossible to fix, we had better prepare ourselves for dealing with mass trauma."

This was no doomsday preacher alarming us to the realities of the approaching apocalypse but one who was in the know about what could happen and what seems inevitable on a broad scale. In 1989 *USA Today* reported, "In the 108-year history of keeping such records, the year 1989 was the worst for disasters. From tornadoes, hurricanes, and earthquakes, more deaths were the result of these than at any other time in our history."[4] Even the workplace is not safe. One researcher notes that 10,500 people die every year because of unsafe work environments.[5] Add to these numbers the AIDS epidemic, violent crimes, divorces, wars, and traumas of unemployment and poverty, and it is no wonder that self-help books sell so well. It is no wonder that the counseling field has so many therapists. We are a traumatized society. We are screaming on the inside. Some are beginning to scream on the outside as well.

As a premed major in college I realized that I had better find out if I would faint at the sight of blood. So one summer I worked in a hospital emergency room. One Friday night after a multiple car accident, ambulances brought in several patients all at once. Everyone seemed to be screaming, so I immediately went toward the one who was screaming the loudest. A seasoned RN grabbed my arm and said, "If they are screaming, they are probably OK. Check that one over there." I checked a man lying motionless and silently on a cart. His pulse was faint and his blood pressure low. We had to do a cut on his ankle to find an uncollapsed vein. By the time we got an IV in a vein, he was dead. He had not been screaming, but he was dying!

The medical illustration may apply to psychic trauma as well. The blows of life hurt us. But often those who hurt most are silent. The screamers are better off than their silent counterparts. At least they know they are hurt and are feeling their pain. For various reasons, we don't allow ourselves to experience the pain we feel. Often others are to blame.

11

They don't want to hear about our pain, or it makes them feel uncomfortable about their own failure to scream, or perhaps it just makes them feel awkward. Therefore, the pain ends up being covered with work, alcohol, sex, drugs, depression, compulsive eating, dieting, and the endless list of acting-out behaviors that indicate to alert observers that all is not well. Having failed to scream, they are now screaming through their disorders, addictions, and compulsions. To scream is normal when facing tragic events. Not to scream may reveal the extent to which we are bleeding to death on the inside.

These difficulties raise a fundamental question as to why we as human beings respond to traumatic events the way we do. What is it about trauma that causes us to respond so? Why does it hit us so hard that it shatters our deepest assumptions about life and reality? These are the questions that the first chapter will seek to address.

It's hard to see clearly with tears in your eyes.
A father after his son's death[1]

Why is light given to him who is in misery,
And life to the bitter of soul,
Who long for death, but it does not come, . . .
Why is light given to a man whose way is hidden . . . ?
Job 3:20–21, 23

CHAPTER 1

Why Traumatic Events Make Us Want to Scream

I t was Saturday morning, August 3. Scores of families, friends, Delta marketing agents, and curious onlookers passed through the Hilton lobby. Our command post for managing the crash crisis had been placed on the second floor mezzanine overlooking the lobby. As I took a break from giving death notifications and working with the Delta and Red Cross personnel, I took some time to grab a cup of coffee and watch the stream of grieving humanity entering the front door of the hotel. Delta Airlines had allowed any relative or friend to board the next available flight to come to Dallas to see if their loved one or friend had been on flight 191. Consequently, when they entered the hotel, most did not know whether their family member or friend was dead or alive, in a hospital, or one of the few who unsnapped their seat belts and walked out of the wreckage of the tail section.[2]

But one man in particular stands out in my mind. I saw him walk into the lobby. He was immaculately dressed in his coordinated dress-for-success business suit. His affluence and success were apparent in every step. He was escorted by a Delta official following a few steps behind. He had already been told that his wife's name had not been on the survivor list. When he got to the registration desk, the usual registration card was placed before him. He drew his expensive pen from his inside coat pocket and printed his name on the first line. The second line was more difficult. He got the city and state, but he couldn't remember his address. Finally, after some time, it came to him. He never put down his phone number; he couldn't remember it. Here was a successful man, a manager of a large corporation, who was used to being in charge, in control, responsible for thousands of details every day. Yet on this particular day he could barely remember his address and phone number. Why? He had suffered a blow, an unexpected and unprepared-for tragedy. Little had he known that when he kissed his wife good-bye the previous morning, it would be a permanent good-bye. This usually competent person had been reduced to being dependent on the Delta agent to get his address and phone number correct. Later, as FBI forms were to be filled out detailing the clothes and jewels his wife had been wearing and naming various scars or birthmarks on her body, the man broke completely. No longer an omnicompetent CEO, he was now broken and screaming.

His response is the more-than-common response to disaster and trauma. But why? How can this reaction be explained? First, it is important to define some terms.

14

Trauma

Our English word *trauma* is derived from a Greek term meaning "wound." This meaning provides a graphic image of what takes place in human trauma. When a person encounters a traumatic experience, he becomes a wounded individual, and as with all wounds there must be a time of healing. However, scarring is often the result. Psychic trauma, as used in professional circles, is defined as "an emotional state of discomfort and stress resulting from memories of an extraordinary, catastrophic experience which shattered the survivor's sense of invulnerability to harm."[3]

In trauma the individual's defense mechanisms break down, and the person can no longer function adequately. Subsequent emotional arousal may even reawaken the traumatic experience to such an extent that there is an attack on the person's defense mechanism from both within and without. The traumatic event, then, collapses the individual's worldview and assumptions about life in one terrific blow.

Life Assumptions Shattered

Our assumptions about how we think life should operate form a cognitive or mental frame around reality. Inside the frame we place our deepest hopes, expectations, and dreams. We see ourselves having a wonderful, successful, and beautiful life. But tragedy breaks the picture. Like a portrait falling off the wall and smashing onto the floor, suddenly the frame that surrounds the beautiful portrait of reality is shattered in pieces. In the case of the man in the lobby, once a self-assured executive, after being informed that his wife was on a plane that had crashed, the picture of his life was suddenly lying on the floor in pieces.

15

The picture we all have about the way we think our lives should be is a composite of our operational theories about life and reality. These assumptions are rarely articulated as such or may not really exist on the conscious level at all, but they are always there. When trauma strikes, the assumptions are challenged and shattered; many get thrown out like the broken frame of the picture. Various researchers have noted that some common assumptions about life in particular are challenged by traumatic events. Epstein writes, "Whether we like it or not, each of us, because he has a human brain, forms a theory of reality that brings order into an otherwise chaotic world of experience. We need a theory to make sense out of the world."[4] It is this theory of the world and self that gets shattered. Our assumptions are formed and proved by much of our life experience; however, when something happens that falls outside the frame of our assumptive world, it throws us for a loop. (See the chart "Circle of Assumptions.")[5] The world is suddenly crazy; it doesn't make sense. The frame cannot contain the picture anymore. All is shattered or at least temporarily put out of order.

The first assumption that is shattered is the assumption of *invulnerability*. On this particular point Janoff-Bulman has observed that "people overestimate the likelihood of their experiencing positive outcomes in life and underestimate the likelihood of experiencing negative events."[6] The result is a shattered worldview when tragic events take place. The individual involved no longer looks at the world as a secure place but now sees it as an evil, unsafe environment in which to live. The innocent diners having lunch at Luby's had their safe world violated when a truck crashed through the window. George Hennard suddenly jumped out of the truck and began mowing down with his nine-millimeter handgun anyone

16

Circle of Assumptions

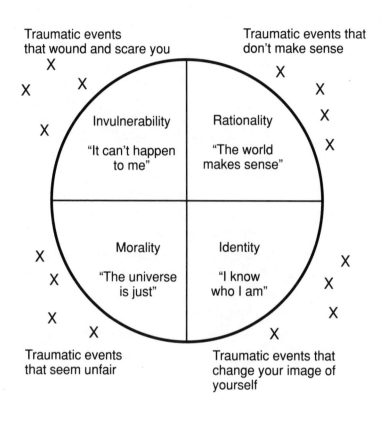

Traumatic events
that wound and scare you

Traumatic events that
don't make sense

Invulnerability

"It can't happen
to me"

Rationality

"The world
makes sense"

Morality

"The universe
is just"

Identity

"I know
who I am"

Traumatic events
that seem unfair

Traumatic events that
change your image of
yourself

who moved. The customers' sense of invulnerability was changed in an instant, probably forever.

While working on this book, I went to my local bank in a Philadelphia suburb. When I went into the lobby to fill out my deposit slip, I noticed that all the pens usually attached to chains were missing. After borrowing a pen from another customer, I proceeded to ask the teller why the pens had disappeared. She replied, "We got robbed yesterday, and the FBI took all the pens for fingerprints." I was a little stunned that this could take place in our secure suburb. I asked her how she felt about being robbed. Her reply was short, succinct, and thoroughly descriptive of the emotional response. She said, "I feel so victimized." Even the world of her workplace was no longer safe. Part of her assumptive world had been shattered. She was feeling the pain of confronting the new reality that she was not an invulnerable person, working at an invulnerable institution. She was very vulnerable. She never dreamed that *her bank* and *her teller's window* would be violated by a robber.[7]

Researchers observe that we are never really prepared for the aftermath of such events. Two such researchers have commented:

Few victims are prepared for the aftermath of victimization, the ways that a crime can echo and reverberate against the rest of the victim's life. The media present crime and its effect in highly structured segments—four column inches of print, thirty minutes of air time. Crime stories have a beginning, middle and end. In dramatizations, the ending is usually happy since the main purpose of these programs is to entertain. Sorrow is overcome, broken bones are mended, criminals are captured and put behind bars—all in the space of sixty minutes. Everything works out all right. These happy endings and formalized structures prepare us for a similar tidiness in reality. We have been reassured, falsely, that the wounds inflicted by crime are time-limited and easily healed.[8]

I don't know why we humans think we are invulnerable. Perhaps as Americans we think it is a constitutional right to have a safe and secure world, a pop interpretation of the pursuit-of-happiness clause. It is certainly commonly observed in teenagers, who usually think they are invulnerable to disease, drugs, accidents, and other tragedies. However, it seems that most of us never entirely grow out of these faulty assumptions. We carry them into our adult lives as well. We are surprised when it is *our* kids who have problems, or when *our* minister gets a divorce, or when *my* husband loses his job, or when the doctor tells me that *I* have a malignant tumor. Our assumption of invulnerability tells us that things like these will never happen to us, even though we can readily admit that they do happen to others. The assumption of invulnerability is an illusion that gets shattered when life does not go our way.

Jon and Stephanie experienced just such a crisis. Living in a large city always raises the possibility of potential harm. But Jon and Stephanie never dreamed about what might happen one Friday night on their way to the grocery store. As newlyweds expecting their first child, they had a bright future until in the parking lot a ski-masked gunman pushed them back into their car and kept them hostage for the next four hours. Constantly making threats to kill them, he placed Jon in the trunk of the car and for the next hours drove through the streets of Baltimore alternating between saying he would let them go and then saying he would kill them. At one point the gunman placed their heads on the dash of the car, pointed the gun at them, and said it was all over for them. Stephanie pleaded for her unborn's life and finally blurted out, "We have lots of money in our bank account." The gunman relented, they drove to an automatic-teller machine, and Stephanie emptied the account. The couple was then dropped off at a nearby train stop, the gunman gave them money for the train (from their own money), and he disappeared. Many sleepless nights immediately followed. Now, seven years later, they still experience flashbacks of the ordeal. Stephanie is especially fearful of ski masks, and Jon, once a very trusting man, has difficulty trusting anyone. What was lost for both on one night in November was their sense of invulnerability. Now when in the city Stephanie always keeps one eye on the crowds. Jon is always aware of someone walking behind him. They now live with a greater sense of their vulnerability.

The same feeling was expressed by a woman after the San Ysidro McDonald's massacre. She wasn't even in the restaurant when James Huberty walked in and opened fire at the employees and customers, killing twenty-one and injuring another fifteen. But as a resident of the community she articulated her reaction: "This world is lost—completely! I feel that anything can happen at any moment. There is danger everywhere; I feel insecure about life; I have more fear now."[9]

The aftermath of trauma also dislodges another basic assumption we all have about life, the assumption of *rationality*. We live our lives assuming that the world is a rational place. It makes sense. There is rhyme and reason to why things happen and why they happen the way they do. Part of this belief is that we expect the world to be understandable and orderly so that we can see how all the parts fit together.

But when tragic events appear from nowhere, they become pieces of a puzzle that don't fit.

The more we try to make sense of the trauma, the more incomprehensible the monstrous event becomes. It defies logic. The assumption that everything should make sense and be understandable is deeply rooted in the human psyche. We are rational beings, the attribute that philosophers through the ages have said separates us from the beast. But when trauma hits, our rationality becomes a curse. We are not like an animal that, after sniffing a dead carcass, can walk off with no apparent feelings of remorse, anger, or regret.[10] Humans are more complex. We are *Homo sapiens* (Latin for "thinking man"). We think about our tragedy, and our thinking can drive us crazy. The replay of the event, the flashbacks, even the smells, bring up reminders of the trauma. As rational beings we seek the rationale in the trauma. When none is found, the traumatic blow is heightened. The meaninglessness of the event can drive one into despair, compulsive activities, abuse of substances, or addictive relationships, which are all possible quick fixes for the pain. All of these feelings illustrate the depth to which our rationality has been attacked and how shattered our world has become. Bard and Sangrey have observed:

> If the world doesn't make sense, people can't do anything with confidence. Victims of personal crime need to find some way of pulling themselves together. They go through a mental process to reorganize and understand the world that has become chaotic. This process helps to reintegrate the violated self, reducing the dissonance caused by its fragmentation.[11]

The senselessness of tragedies can work in many directions. Mike and Marilyn Steinberg were two of the few survivors of the Delta 191 crash. They walked away from the crash site with minor bruises and burns. Even their luggage survived without a scratch, and none of their contents were damaged. Passengers in the seats in front and on one side perished. But they walked away. Why? The why question is raised on both sides of the hall in the Dallas-Fort Worth Hilton. In one room a father is asking why his young-adult daughter, on her way to start her first job after college, was killed. The Steinbergs ask why were they left alive. But both are functioning as rational human beings, asking the ultimate question about the meaning of things. But their question lands in empty space. No answer is sufficient, or so it seems. These grievers and survivors are not asking an intellectual question as in a freshman Philosophy 101 class. They are raging at the world, God, Delta, even me as a chaplain, because they cannot understand the utterly incomprehensible. No, their question is not intellectual; it is emotional, rooted in the fabric of their very being. Life is supposed to make sense, but the loss of life, home, limb, job, self-esteem, or one's future is irrational. The irrationality makes the trauma even more difficult and compounds our inability to scream.

In commenting again about crime victims, Bard and Sangrey noted, "Identifying a cause, however rational or irrational, gives people a sense of order and predictability in their lives. People do not want to believe that things happen randomly; they want to believe that they happen *because*. . . . "[12] Even Viktor Frankl, writing from his perspective as a Nazi-death-camp survivor, said, "In some way, suffering ceases to be suffering at the moment it finds a meaning."[13] Such is this drive toward regaining rationality when trauma hits.

This drive toward regaining some control through understanding takes many paths. Some blame themselves for what happened; others blame others (as in blaming the air-traffic controllers in the Delta crash); some say, "They got what they deserved" or "They shouldn't have been flying," or "Why were you in *that* part of the city?" All of these statements are initial attempts to bring some rationality to the irrationality of traumatic events. It has been noted that even the illusion of mental control is often enough for victims to regain some sense of rationality. Therapists note:

> It can be harmful (and it is surely insensitive) for other people to insist that the victim be rational during the impact stage of the crisis. The best support is provided by those who are able to listen, hearing out the victim's notions about the reason for the crime and supporting the need to make them.[14]

When trauma hits, reason goes out the window. This compounds the scream. But another part of our assumptive world is thrown into confusion. When the picture of reality smashes to the floor, the victim's sense of *morality* is also greatly affected. Just as we expect our world to be a rational place, we also expect it to be just and fair. We expect good guys to be rewarded and bad guys to be punished. However, traumatic events cause the good guy/bad guy philosophy to be tossed to the wind. It no longer seems valid in the face of irrational and undeserved torture. Job in the Bible may have been one of the first in early recorded history to raise the issue of justice in the face of his own pain:

> "If I cry out concerning wrong,
>   I am not heard.
> If I cry aloud,
>   there is no justice" (Job 19:7).

Our expectation that life be fair toward us is one of the primary assumptions that frame reality for us. Whether it is a violent crime, or losing a loved one through death, or finding oneself unemployed, the response is the same. This should not happen to us; it is not fair. No matter how sinful or unworthy the person may consciously consider himself, when tragedy occurs, violence is done to the human spirit. This violence is experienced as an unjust intrusion into the life of the victim. An injustice has been suffered, and the human spirit rages in torment against the unseen and seen forces that may be to blame. Ultimately, God is blamed for being unable to prevent the psychic crime or for being completely passive toward the violence. Oxford professor C. S. Lewis wrote after the death of his wife:

> Where is God? This is one of the most disquieting symptoms. When you are happy, so happy that you have no sense of needing Him, so happy that you are tempted to feel His claims upon you as an interruption, if you remember yourself and turn to Him with gratitude and praise, you will be—or so it feels— welcomed with open arms. But go to Him when your need is desperate, when all other help is vain, and what do you find? A door slammed in your face, and a sound of bolting and double bolting on the inside. After that, silence. You may as well turn away. The longer you wait, the more emphatic the silence will become. There are no lights in the windows. It might be an empty house. Was it ever inhabited? It seemed so once. And that seeming was as strong as this. What can this mean? Why is He so present a commander in our time of prosperity and so very absent a help in time of trouble?[15]

When this "silence in heaven" happens to people of faith, often entire religious belief systems are brought into conflict.

For many the trauma produces a second crisis, a crisis of faith and a total reevaluation of their religious experience. Janoff-Bulman has noted that often the greater the degree of "untested convictions," the greater the shattering of the belief:

> To the extent that particular assumptions are held with extreme confidence and have not been challenged, they are more likely to be utterly shattered, with devastating results for the victim. . . . Similarly, basic assumptions that have not been questioned may shatter most easily and lead to the greatest psychological disruption. Thus, if an individual strongly believes that the world is truly a benevolent place, this assumption will be easily destroyed by the experience of victimization, and the process of rebuilding is apt to be a difficult one.[16]

Certainly, the historic Judeo-Christian tradition does not present a worldview that is singularly benevolent. However, many of its adherents still have the popular opinion that they should be free from any inherent evil that can always be lurking around the corner. This is probably explained by the first assumption of invulnerability. But the reality still stands, when trauma hits home, it is usually seen as terribly unfair and raises a host of moral issues for the victim. One Catholic priest confesses that even the leadership of the church is not prepared for the realities that suffering brings:

> It is a painful fact indeed to realize how poorly prepared most Christian leaders are to be when they are invited to be spiritual leaders in the true sense. Most of them are used to thinking in terms of large-scale organizations, getting people together in churches, schools, and hospitals, and running the

show as a circus director. They have become unfamiliar with, and even somewhat afraid of, the deep and significant movements of the spirit. I am afraid that in a few decades the Church will be accused of having failed in its most basic task: to offer men creative ways to communicate with the source of human life.[17]

In the absence of understanding from church leadership the logical conclusion is that God is the real source of the injustice. One young mother who lost a five-year-old daughter in a car accident said that even though she still attended church and was involved in many church programs, she could not bring herself to address God in prayer. To her, God had become morally unjust for allowing her innocent daughter to die such an untimely death. Her reaction was no longer to talk to the One who was responsible. Often these tragedies reveal the naive faith we have had, naive on the experiential side of the ledger. Nouwen observed, "When Christianity is reduced to an all-encompassing ideology, nuclear man is all too prone to be skeptical about its relevance to his life experience."[18]

In many faith traditions the focus is on embracing intellectual beliefs, often to the neglect of a counterbalancing emphasis on the role of experience. When the beliefs clash with the experience encountered in traumatic events, the beliefs are shown to be somewhat shallow and dysfunctional. The trauma can push our religious belief systems in two different directions. Studies have shown that survivors of the Holocaust and of the atom-bomb blasts in Japan went in two opposing, extreme directions. For many Jewish survivors, the death-of-God doctrine developed as their explanation for the silence of God in their torment. Elie Wiesel, the Nobel Peace Prize chronicler of the Holocaust, said that for him,

God died the night he watched a young boy hanged to death by the Nazis. His graphic diary details his steps to the death of God in his life:

> The three victims mounted together onto the chairs. The three necks were placed at the same moment within the nooses. "Long live liberty!" cried the two adults. But the child was silent. "Where is God? Where is He?" someone behind me asked. At a sign from the head of the camp, the three chairs tipped over. Total silence throughout the camp. On the horizon, the sun was setting. "Bare your heads!" yelled the head of the camp. His voice was raucous. We were weeping. "Cover your head!" Then the march past began. The two adults were no longer alive.... But the third rope was still moving; being so light, the child was still alive.... Behind me, I heard the same man asking: "Where is God now?" And I heard a voice within me answer him: "Where is He?" Here He is—He is hanging here on this gallows.[19]

Later, Wiesel alluded to this experience as the time when his faith was consumed forever.[20]

A Japanese woman wrestled with the two extremes following the nuclear explosion she survived. She confessed:

> At the moment we all become completely separated human beings. Seeing those wretched figures of people, I felt great pity and having experienced such a terrible state of living hell, I thought there is no God, no Buddha, there is no God . . . no help.

But after a while her feelings changed. She observed,

> As time passed and the world became peaceful . . . I began to feel that we owe everything to God. . . . I cannot attribute the

fact that I was not killed to my own power. I believed that God ordered me to put on a pair of sandals [which saved her life].[21]

When the bombs of life hit us, our worldview is shattered. Our assumption of a fair world run by a benevolent deity is brought into direct conflict with the hell of our pain. Experiencing pain brings about a change in how we view ourselves. The picture of reality that was once so beautiful was not something detached from who I am. The picture was a self-portrait. The picture is me. The shattering of my assumptions ultimately is the shattering of my self-identity, of how I view myself.

The last assumption that is affected extremely by trauma is that of *self-identity*. We all carry a picture of ourselves in our heads if not in our wallets. This picture may not be as pleasing to us as we would like it to be, but it is who we are. We may think it would look better if we lost a few pounds or worked out more or had fewer blemishes. But for the most part, the picture we have of ourselves is that of being able to get up every morning, carry out our responsibilities, function through the day, and have some distinctive capabilities and assets. We all have things we don't like about ourselves, but most of us see ourselves as capable, functioning individuals having some worth and merit. However, the trauma of victimization changes all this. Janoff-Bulman again has observed:

The experience of being victimized leads to serious questioning of these self-perceptions. The trauma of victimization activates negative self-images in the victim. Victims see themselves as weak, helpless, needy, frightened, and out of control. . . . The victimization is neither expected nor intended by them. They perceive themselves as powerless and helpless in the face of forces beyond their control. . . . In addition to weakness and powerlessness, victims are apt to experience a sense of deviance. After all, they have been singled out for misfortune and this establishes them as different from other people. The self-perception of deviance no doubt serves to reinforce negative images of oneself as unworthy and weak.[22]

The self-perception has changed. Now the individual who once carried on with a healthy sense of self views herself differently. She sees herself as a victim, and if a victim once, then possibly again. Having been singled out without any rhyme or reason leads one to a different self-perception. As the researcher explained above, this new sense of deviance (not necessarily in the negative sense) affects how one approaches life and relationships.

It explains why the Vietnam veteran, seeing himself as unworthy of love, sabotages his marriage through violence or drinking so that his wife finally leaves. It explains why some very moral and religious people greatly alter their convictions and develop illicit relationships or start drinking for the first time. If they are different (deviant), then to maintain the new identity, they begin to act out the new self-perception. It is all below the level of articulated consciousness, but it is still there, driving much of what the sufferer is experiencing.

Some Israeli researchers have noted that this change in fundamental identity issues is due to a collapse of the entire self-structure:

Psychic trauma . . . is the collapse of the structure of self along four referential planes resulting from an encounter of a catastrophic threat and a chaotic response. . . . The traumatic experience, once occurring, cannot be integrated into the structure of self and meaning, and hinders the continuation of the autonomous functions of the structure.[23]

This means that the sense of wholeness and integration that we all have within ourselves has been lost. We can no longer see how our life fits into the larger world with any significant meaning and purpose. Who we are in the world has been lost and shattered. Not only has the frame around the picture of ourselves been altered, but also the picture itself is now different or gone. We look into the frame and see nothing. We have lost our bearings, our boundaries, and our complete sense of who we are. This loss is devastating. Not to know who we are when so much of our lives has fallen apart is almost as painful as the original trauma that produced all the effects. The Israeli researchers again noted, "The central feature of the traumatic experience is the final horrible 'realization' that the rules that define the individual's identity and reality are not operational anymore."[24]

If we don't know who we are, how can we function or go on? Chapter 3 will focus on the courageous reality that many do go on and learn many helpful things that facilitate healing in the process. But before looking at what we have learned from the walking wounded, it may be helpful to visualize clearly what a traumatized person looks like. Many are walking around today who, like the unconscious, dying man in the emergency room, do not recognize the emotional bleeding on the inside. Individuals may wear coats and ties, makeup, and smiles; but underneath the masquerade of appearance lies a lingering reservoir of pain. Their world has been shattered, their very personhood attacked, their assumptions fractured, but they go to work, earn livings, go to church, have relationships, and keep on parenting, in spite of the hidden pain and silent screams that torment and deaden the savor of life experiences daily. What does this traumatized person look like? Read on. . . .

Out of the wound we pluck the shrapnel
Thorns we squeeze out of the hand.
Even poison forth we suck, and after the pain we ease.

But images that grow within the soul have life
Like cancer often cut, live on below the deepest of the knife
Waiting their time to shoot at some defenceless hour
Their poison, unimpaired, at the heart's root

And, like a golden shower, unanswerably sweet,
Bright with returning guilt, fatally in moment's time
Defeat our brazen towers long-built;

And all our former pain and all our surgeon's care
Is lost, and all the unbearable (in vain borne once)
Is still to bear.[1]

C. S. Lewis
"Relapse"

Whether 'tis nobler in the mind to suffer
The slings and arrows of outrageous fortune,
Or to take arms against a sea of troubles,
And by opposing end them?
William Shakespeare
Hamlet[2]

CHAPTER 2

What a Traumatized Person Looks Like

The popular way of visualizing a traumatized person is the Hollywood version of an airplane disaster film. The airplane develops a mechanical problem en route to its destination, and when the passengers are told to prepare for a crash landing, panic breaks out. Women and children scream, faint, or pray. Men shout, "What in thunder is going on?" But that's Hollywood! The common, popular vision about trauma seems to picture screaming people running every which way, stampeding over others to get away from impending danger.

Studies of disaster seem to reveal much the opposite picture.[3] People appear frozen and calm, often doing very heroic things. In the MGM fire in Las Vegas a man risked his life to go back into a smoky hallway to see if a man in a wheelchair he had seen earlier was still in his room. We all remember seeing the footage of the man in the Potomac River, a survivor of the Air Florida crash, who repeatedly gave the helicopter life rope to others rather than save himself. The icy waters finally took his life while he was saving others. In 1988 at Flugtag 88 the crack Italian *Frecce Tricolori* put on a spectacular air show at Ramstein Air Force Base, Germany. In the finale the spectacle turned to catastrophe when two of the jets collided over the field. Seventy people were killed, with hundreds injured, in the fireball and falling debris. At the site were twenty-one medical personnel from the Ramstein clinic and the Otterberg Red Cross. Their tent was located fifteen meters from where the fireball settled. Were there panic and mass hysteria among these personnel? One of the medics remembers:

I'll never fully know what happened at Aid Station B that horrible day. Just what forces were at work—training, character, bravery—in its individual members which brought order to chaos even as the fatal fireball began its heavenward journey. But order did immediately assert itself. None of the team— American or German—ran away. They stayed, even though they had been directly threatened by death and continued to be threatened by the egress rockets (for seat ejection) still in

Col. Nutareilli's plane. That nucleus of brave folks served to draw victims and other selfless individuals to their aid. . . . If war is the great proving ground for such sainthood then Flugtag 88 was war, for I saw saints that day.[4]

No, the research on trauma presents a somewhat different picture than what is often assumed. This is what makes the aspect of screaming so difficult and facilitates the failure to scream for many. We don't recognize the screaming of others because we have very different notions about what traumatized persons should look like.

Psychiatric Diagnosis

The standard textbook in the mental-health community for evaluating and diagnosing all mental-health disorders is DSM III. DSM III stands for *Diagnostic and Statistical Manual of Mental Disorders*, third edition. (A revision is currently under way.) The category of posttraumatic-stress disorder (PTSD), chronic or delayed (309.81) says:

The essential feature is the development of characteristic symptoms following a psychologically traumatic event that is generally outside the range of usual human experience. The characteristic symptoms involve reexperiencing the traumatic event; numbing of responsiveness to, or reduced involvement with, the external world; and a variety of autonomic, dysphoric or cognitive symptoms.[5]

This definition is saying that the traumatized person has been numbed to life. He or she is not necessarily erratic or outwardly violent but characterized more by an overall "flat" or numb appearance. While working as an emergency-room technician, I witnessed a college-age student calmly walk into

35

the hospital with his own finger in hand. He had cut it off while trying to fix a lawn mower. He wasn't outwardly upset or even in pain but merely walked up to the nurses' station and announced, "I need to see a doctor; I just cut off my finger!" He was numb. This is normal. Six months or so later, if he were still numb and so calm, we would diagnose him as having PTSD.

Following the Delta crash, I received a call almost six months to the date after the tragedy. It was one of the Delta employees I had gotten to know very well through our hectic week of caring for the families. She told me about one of their employees who was not doing well and wondered if I could see the individual. The following week the man arrived and described his past several months. He couldn't sleep, he had recurring dreams of the crash, his alcohol intake had gone up, and he was experiencing severe marital conflict with his wife. He told me he felt that he was just going through the motions of life; he really wasn't there; it was as if he were always watching his own life. When I asked him what he had done in the crash, he told me that he was in charge of the group who had removed the remains from the tail section of the aircraft. Since the L1011 had slammed into the water tanks head on, everything was thrown back into the only remaining section of the aircraft, the tail section. He then recounted for me what he had seen as he crawled back into the tail section to look for any human remains. Amid the aeronautical debris, cosmetics, news magazines, and other personal effects were body parts. His dreams at night were videos reliving and reviewing what he had seen in those moments of doing his job. As a result, he was now numb, numb in his relationship with his wife, numb at work, numb with his kids.

To try to relax his mind and rid his brain of the memories

of looking at human remains, he increased his drinking. The only thing that wasn't numb, his mind, he tried to numb with alcohol. But his strategy wasn't working. He was beginning to scream. I asked what was normal for a human being to experience when he sees the dissociated parts of another human being. He said that he didn't know. I said, "To scream, weep, cry. A violence has been done to place you in a situation in which you had to look at something so inhuman. But you were doing your job, and besides, men don't scream or cry. So we bury the pain, hoping that it will go away or that it can be numbed or removed with Johnny Walker."

This man was an innocent victim of doing his job. He had to look upon things no human should have to see and was suffering severely because of it. Employers, often not realizing the psychological dimensions of such events, can't understand why employees can't move on afterward. Their attitude only contributes to the problem and reveals how unknowledgeable most of us are about what a traumatized person looks like. We assume that if one can still work and is not overly agitated, then he or she is OK.

The Delta employee also illustrates a second element of what a person in trauma looks like. DSM III states:

> The traumatic event can be reexperienced in a variety of ways. Commonly the individual has recurrent painful, intrusive recollections of the event or recurrent dreams or nightmares during which the event is reexperienced. In rare instances there are dissociativelike states, lasting from a few minutes to several hours or even days, during which components of the event are relived and the individual behaves as though experiencing the event at that moment. . . . A person may complain of feeling detached or estranged from other people, that he or she has lost the ability to become interested in previously enjoyed

significant activities, or that the ability to feel emotions of any type, especially those associated with intimacy, tenderness, and sexuality, is markedly decreased.[6]

In December of 1985 a chartered U.S. Army jetliner crashed in Gander, Newfoundland, killing all on board. As the elite corps of the army the 101st Army Airborne Division entered a corporate grief process. Of the 248 soldiers killed, 189 were members of a single battalion. Hence, one whole battalion (110) was lost in one crash. For weeks following the crash, members of the division experienced many of the above symptoms. The most frequently observed initial manifestations among the remaining unit members were their numbness and their going-though-the-motions reactions. Recurring dreams were common, in which individuals would see buddies in the flames of the crash. Some even experienced "ghost reactions," seeing fellow soldiers who were on the plane in the dining hall and around the base. One survivor experienced an extreme panic reaction when he mistakenly identified a new soldier on base as one who was killed.[7] Incest and rape victims cite similar experiences. Periodic intrusions of the painful events into daily experiences may be triggered by a particular smell (after-shave or cigarette smoke) or by being touched in a particular way. One Vietnam veteran told me that just the smell of jet fuel brought back to his mind all the experiences of Vietnam. This made it difficult for him to fly or go near airports, where the smell is usually present.

One of my students told me of a time when hunting with his World War II-vintage father. As they approached a ridge overlooking a particular river, suddenly his father stopped and froze for a moment. Then he said, "I can't believe it is still here after forty years." His adult son asked, "What do you mean?" The father replied, "This place reminds me of a spot during our invasion of Germany from the French side. We crossed a river much like this one, but the Germans were waiting for us on the other side. We lost half our men that day to the Germans." Viewing the river with a gun in his hand had brought it all back. He later told his son, "The older I get, the more the pain of that moment hurts."[8] Yes, buried are the painful moments of life, but they are never forgotten. They are still very much a part of us, a part of who we are, whether or not we acknowledge them. A smell, a sight, a similarity can bring it all back in one intrusive video flashback. So permanently embedded are these memories that I am told by actor friends that they are taught to cry on cue by consciously bringing back painful memories when the script demands an emotional response. The great Russian theoretician Stanislavsky trained drama students to find and use to their advantage this hidden grief and pain.[9] He knew what many today have not realized. We never totally walk away from our pain. It is always there, waiting for the right similarity or circumstance to arrive in order to raise its ugly head and remind us that denial has not removed its existence.

Other symptoms that are also associated with posttraumatic stress disorder are: excessive arousal, such as hyper-alertness; exaggerated startle response; and difficulty falling asleep. Some complain of impaired memory or difficulty in concentrating or completing tasks. In the case of life-threatening trauma shared with others, survivors often describe painful guilt feelings about surviving when many did not or about the things they had to do in order to survive.[10] The movie *Sophie's Choice* centers on this theme. As a Jewish woman with two children, in order to survive, the protagonist had to choose which of her two children would be given up to the extermination camps. The rest of her life she was tormented by her own survivor guilt and the choice she made. Whether it is an air crash, or war experience, or a hostage situation in which one woman is molested and another one isn't, the response can produce the typical survival whys. All these reactions are normal responses to abnormal situations.

If anything, what the DSM III definition does is normalize what often appears as very unusual behaviors. When a spouse is awakened to her mate's startle reactions while sleeping or an employer wonders what's wrong with Ralph when he daydreams at work, these reactions may be normal responses to the traumatic events they have experienced. They appear uncommon to the untrained eye, but to someone who understands the nature of traumatic events, they are normal reactions. One Desert Stormer, a reservist, returned home to work in his hardware store. Family and friends began to notice that he had never taken off his combat boots. When asked what I thought about it, I responded that it probably depends on what happened to him in the conflict. I was told that this particular individual was part of a transportation company that was keeping the tanks refueled during a flanking movement to cut off the Iraqi forces. In the middle of the night a flare was sent up, and to the dismay of this truck driver, Iraqi soldiers were next to the truck with guns raised. He opened his M16 and quickly snuffed out about twenty Iraqis. The next morning he got a closer look. Taking their guns and ammo, he saw pictures of wives and children on the bodies. One week he was running a hardware store in New York, and the next week he found himself going through the remains of twenty human beings who were no longer alive because of his well-trained instinctive reaction. The boots were part of hanging on to or acting out the pain that he probably had buried. He was back in New York, but his psyche would say that he was screaming. Screaming is the normal reaction to taking a life, even when one's own life is on the line.

Another man told me of his difficulty in really committing himself to the company he worked for. A history of firings and bosses who did not fulfill their promises revealed a pattern of the sequential trauma of unemployment and work-related problems. What appeared to bosses as "an inability to commit" or "a lack of loyalty" was perhaps a normal response to what has unfortunately become a normal event in American society. The man's distrust of hierarchy and leadership was perhaps a mild form of detachment in response to the repeated trauma of unemployment and lying by employers. What appeared as disloyalty to an employer was the normal reaction to a series of abnormal blows suffered by one individual.

In summary, this section has tried to clarify how the traumatized person can be recognized. For diagnostic purposes or for loved ones trying to understand a friend or relative, four main criteria must be observed.

A Recognizable Stressor

First, there must exist a recognizable stressor (an unusual catastrophic or traumatic event) that is out of the ordinary enough to evoke the rest of the symptoms.

I attended a professional-society meeting for mental-health counselors. In one small group the facilitator asked each of us to reveal why we were part of this particular society (the Society for Traumatic-Stress Studies). One woman psychiatrist responded by saying that after twenty years of practice she wanted to evaluate her files of all the people she had treated to look for commonalities. She said she finally realized that most of her emotionally disturbed and mentally ill patients had one common factor: traumatic events in their childhood, adolescence, or early-adult years. She finally blurted out, "I'm not sure I believe in mental illness anymore. It seems that these mentally ill people have not adequately recovered from the traumatic events in their lives." [11] In my own counseling I have seen this same phenomenon. Many things fall into place once the question about traumatic events in their lives is raised. By the way, some counselors do not ask such questions in their initial workup and often miss significant clues to understanding the abnormal behavior that has brought the person into the counselor's office.

I had one such couple in counseling for many sessions. They were both from ethnic backgrounds, and the husband had a lot of anger and at times got violent with his wife. Finally, she couldn't handle it any longer and came to see me. Initially, I tried to find the usual causes of such anger but found no apparent reason for his violent temper and extreme raging. After a couple of sessions of seeing her, she dropped a clue: "Al has been a locked box ever since he returned from 'nam." It changed my whole approach. In my next meeting with Al I asked him about Vietnam, whether he had seen much action, whether he had seen buddies blown away, or whether he had done some things he was ashamed of. In very explicit words, he told me that Vietnam was none of my business since I hadn't been there. 1 agreed with his wife. Al was a locked box. Something was locked inside him about Vietnam, but he wasn't about to let me in. However, a spillover effect was creating immense problems in his marriage and the relationships he said he valued most. They are now divorced, and as far as I know, Al still has the secrets of Vietnam safely secured in his emotionally locked box. But the same box that locks pain in locks people out . . . one of whom was his wife and the other a counselor! Trauma affects people greatly. Much of what counselors call mental illness may in fact be the lingering effects of significant damage caused by major stressors in their lives.

One study done by the Saint Louis University Medical Center found a significantly high proportion of severely disturbed individuals with prior traumatic events. Ninety-eight percent of those with multiple-personality disorder had some type of either physical, sexual, or psychological abuse. Eighty-one percent had incest in their backgrounds. Of these, 92 percent suffered from amnesia, and 45 percent were depressive.[12]

When we look at people's lives and find such recognizable stressors, then it is reasonable to assume that we are dealing with a traumatized person. Don't get the wrong idea. Trauma does not have to be a single, one-time, uncommon tragedy. Certainly, war, rape, incest, air crashes, being a victim of crime, and suffering the loss of a loved one are traumatic events. But so are "smaller" traumas that have an accumulative effect over time. The well-known Holmes Stress Scale[13] operates under the assumption that a collection of stressors over time amounts to a high degree of trauma. Also, repeated traumas of the same sort, although individually not traumatic, with the second or third exposure become high on the stress scale. Illustrations include multiple deaths in a short period of time or repeated theft of property or personal effects. Each of these produces pronounced feelings of violation. Bard and Sangrey have observed:

> Burglary involves extensions of the self but it is more grievous than purse snatching because the offender has violated the home of the victim. Most people feel their homes to be places of refuge and safety, shelters from the dangerous outside. . . . Burglary victims often feel this intrusion much more deeply than the property loss they suffer.[14]

Even the theft of one's car can produce an extreme sense of loss because of the value we place on the automobile in our society. For many the car is a more important extension of themselves than their own homes.[15] In the final analysis, it is sometimes difficult to evaluate what is traumatic and what isn't or, putting it another way, what should or should not be traumatic. What is traumatic to one person may not be traumatic to another. The question will be addressed later in the book as to why some apparently have greater dispositions to surviving these critical-incident stresses of life.

Reexperiencing the Trauma

The second way to recognize a traumatized person is when the individual's mind repeatedly replays pictures of the event. A father who lost his five-year-old daughter in a car accident told me of the intrusions into his mind of the scene of his daughter's being hit by the car. It replayed over and over again in his mind—while he was at work, in his dreams, while driving the car. They always ended with the same feeling of what he could have done to prevent her death. With time they were not as frequent, but still the right image or event could bring back the recollection quickly.

Studies of rape victims have shown that this visual replay is a common characteristic of their experience.[16] As alluded to earlier, even the smell of the rapist's after-shave or other smells or sounds can trigger the replay mechanism in the mind. One woman confessed that she lost her taste for pizza after her sexual violation. Her attacker had pizza on his breath, and her mind now easily makes the mental leap from the smell of pizza to the association of pizza with sexual violence.

One pilot in the Gulf War was surprised that the images of soldiers running for cover had become a permanent videotape replaying in his dreams. He had dropped his bombs on many targets, but on one occasion, while looking through his heads-up display, he saw real, live people on the Iraqi gunship he was about to knock out. As he released his missiles and banked sharply, he saw these humans running for cover. For him the war had changed. These were no longer targets on some sophisticated video game but people ... people with wives, families, histories. The mental tape would not erase. It was there, carefully recorded by his brain. His confession was the beginning of his scream. His scream showed that he was human and was experiencing posttraumatic stress as a result.[17]

A more severe form of this replay is when the person literally acts as if or feels as if he is experiencing the traumatic event. We have seen the scenes in several recovering-Vietnam-veteran movies. The veteran, back in civilian life, hears a helicopter overhead and suddenly freaks out, hits the dirt, and thinks he is back in Vietnam. These are extreme forms of the mental recollection, but they do exist. Often these responses demand some very special attention by professional care-givers.

Numbing and Reduced Responsiveness

As mentioned earlier, the earliest response to trauma is the overall numbing that sets in. An individual's defense system takes over to buy time and help him adjust to the extreme nature of the stressor that seeks to tear apart his psychological well-being. The numbing has a spillover effect, creating a certain diminished interest in the usual activities of life. The person may feel detached or estranged from those he loves most. Psychologists talk about the "flat affect" that characterizes this symptom. The facial posture is flat and unresponsive. There is no twinkle in the eye, and it is as if the eyes have become hollow or vacant.

While talking about this chapter with my wife, she humorously reminded me that this is the way most men appear! I believe that she is correct. Many men are walking around today, having been wounded by divorces, unaffirming fathers, unreasonable and unfair bosses, and being fired. The very life has been taken out of them, and they are traumatized by the multiple but unacknowledged pains they have experienced. The result is a "flat affect." Their affections are dead, and they are virtually unresponsive. The trauma, of course, is not gender-specific. Women have theirs too, but sometimes they are better articulators of their pain and are much more willing to discuss their pain with others than men are.

Two or More Symptoms at the Same Time

The final professional criterion for recognizing a person undergoing the effects of trauma is having at least two of the following: hyperalertness or exaggerated startle response, sleep disturbance, guilt about surviving when others have not or about behavior required for survival, memory impairment or trouble concentrating, avoidance of activities that arouse recollection of the traumatic event, and intensification of symptoms by exposure to events that symbolize or resemble the traumatic event.[18]

Know anybody who looks like this? Even as I write these words, I can still see many of these symptoms in myself. There are times I feel so beaten up by life that I feel as if I am just an observer rather than a participant in life. I can feel myself pulling away from people because of the pain experienced in the past. We develop certain strategies to help us survive the pain of life. These work for a while, but then we begin to pay a price in our inner and eventually our outer lives. When we begin to feel our pain, we are beginning to do the screaming we should have done much earlier. As we confess and share our pain, we begin to release the demons that have kept our pain hidden and bottled up.

Yes, something in life has probably traumatized most of us. In lay terms I describe these responses in three areas: First, trauma brings about an initial shock. The shock includes the numbness, certain denial mechanisms, sometimes fantasy withdrawal, and sometimes hysteria. Following this initial shock, the normal emotional releases follow. These may include anger, depression, sobbing, even praying and/or bargaining with God. After the emotional releases, more behavioral processes begin to play an important role. These processes are the beginning attempts to cope with the reality of the loss and what happened. It may involve going back to work, or throwing out the clothes of the lost loved one, or having sex for the first time after being raped. These processes may or may not be satisfactory attempts. More probably than not, they will be painful attempts and unsatis-factory. It will be much later when work, enjoying our rela-tionships, being at home, or having a normal sex life will be restored. The final phase of these reactions is the cognitive or intellectual processes whereby we begin to reason or think differently about what has happened in the trauma. Here there may be a need for someone to help us sort out the faulty reasoning we may have had about life in the past. It is here that the reframing mentioned earlier becomes vitally important. Without this new mental picture of what happened to us, final acceptance, adjustment, and healing are very difficult.[19]

It may be helpful in closing this chapter to distinguish what many have called the stages of grief from the character-istics of a traumatized person mentioned in this chapter. The name usually associated with these stages of grief is Elisa-beth Kubler-Ross. Though she is probably the one who has popularized the field most, she is certainly not the first or only important researcher on the subject of grief and loss. Through the process of being with many hundreds of dying patients, researchers have begun to understand the common stages or reactions to one's own loss of health and subse-quent decline and death. Since traumatic-stress reactions are sometimes similar to these death-and-dying reactions, the stages may be helpful to outline. Also, since traumatic events usually involve the loss of life or loss of some sort, these reactions are often very much a part of the traumatic-stress reactions.

Ross's classic five grief reactions are denial, anger, bargaining with God, depression, and acceptance.[20] She viewed these reactions as initial coping mechanisms in which the terminally ill patient reacts to his own knowledge of death and dying. It reveals a forward movement leading toward the final full acceptance of the implications of his death. At the acceptance stage the patient has made peace with his own death and, for the present, can continue to live with this acceptance with meaning, purpose, and full cognition.

Another researcher likens these stages more to dramas. The grief reactions that a traumatized person initially experiences is a series of dramas in which either healthy or unhealthy responses help the person or hinder the person in his forward progress. Nighswonger has outlined six dramas that characterize this movement: shock, emotion, negotiation, cognition, commitment, and completion.[21] The healthy response to shock is denial. This frames denial perhaps in a more positive light than denial is sometimes cast. Denial, then, is necessary for true forward movement through the trauma mine field. The unhealthy response to shock is panic. In Nighswonger's development the healthy response to emotion is catharsis and anger; the unhealthy responses are depression, guilt, and shame. Again, this scheme normalizes the emotions of venting and anger, while putting depression, guilt, and shame in more negative terms. In the negotiation phase bargaining is healthy, while selling out or withdrawing is unhealthy. Often the experience of Job in the Bible is cast as a self-righteous person wrestling with God about his undeserved disease. However, Nighswonger would see this more as normative reactions. Merely to give in and thank God for a disease for the learning experience of it or any other justification is unthinkable in terms of current research.[22] In the cognition drama a realistic hope and search for meaning are healthy responses, while bitterness, despair, and gloom are unhealthy ones. The commitment drama sees acceptance as healthy and mere resignation as unhealthy.

Often resignation may be viewed as acceptance. Many have resigned to the fact that a loved one may die or never recover but may not have fully accepted the reality or the ultimate meaning of this in terms of their own lives. Resignation continues to breed bitterness, while acceptance can move one on to fulfillment.

The final drama sets the healthy response of fulfillment against the unhealthy reaction of forlornness. Forlornness, as used in this way, describes one being left behind, deserted and without hope. It is typified by the expression "I can't go on." One professor, after the long, declining illness and death of his wife, did not show up to teach for many days. After someone was sent to his house, it was discovered that he had taken his own life. After the long illness and death of his wife he had become forlorn. He couldn't go on. Without his wife he was deserted and obviously felt there was nothing else to live for.

The opposite of forlornness is fulfillment . . . fulfillment in the sense that something fills the person as a result of the traumatic experience. Many new insights, skills, relationships, even careers emerge from the disasters of life. Elie Wiesel, mentioned earlier, has made a career of being a chronicler of his Holocaust experience. His near-death experience and the observed death of millions gave him a life purpose . . . a life to fulfill.

A common question that arises when looking at the concept of stages or grief dramas is whether they are chronological. Does one always enter at the same place and then progressively move through the stages sequentially and without regression? I feel that the stage or drama concept is helpful in terms of recognizing where a person is in her own grief experience, but I do not believe that these stages are necessarily chronological or predictive in terms of what each person *should* experience. Therese Rando concludes:

> Some caregivers who have believed stages to be invariant have responded to the dying or mourners in terms of the stages they were supposed to be in rather than their individual needs at that point in time. They have tried to fit the individual to the theory instead of using the theory to gain a better understanding of the individual. Not all people will have the same experience, need the same interventions, or follow the same clinical course.[23]

The stages are more *logical* than *chronological*. From my experience as a disaster chaplain, I have observed that people enter at various stages. Some people storm into the grief arena yelling and screaming at anything that moves. They are angry, and they are letting the world, God, and all humans on the planet know it. Others enter quietly in either a silent denial or depression. After the Delta crash some wanted to go to the crash site to see if they could find their loved ones. They believed the person to be alive even after death notifications had been made. Others held on to the belief that their relatives hadn't been on the plane even after the medical examiners had positive identifications. They were still in very strong denial. One policeman became an activist in working through his denial by playing policeman for his dead mother. Using his fraternal order of police connections, he tried to get the inside scoop on a cover-up in how the medical examinations were taking place and to learn why bodies weren't going to be released as soon as he would like.

In the early stages I observed many initial emotional reactions. When I first drove up to the Dallas-Fort Worth Hilton, I noticed a man walking around the grounds crying. I put my arm around him and asked if I could walk with him. Sobbing, he told me that he had lost his "baby," a twenty-year-old daughter. Others wanted to sue Delta and were contacting attorneys. They had the need to find blame, arising from their legitimate anger at the situation. Throughout the week following the crash, I began to see how people could work through the various stages and reactions even in such a short time. I saw individuals move from bargaining with God, to anger, to depression, back to original denial, and by the end of the week, to a certain acceptance of the reality of the loss. At the end of the week a Japanese-American male who had lost his wife and only daughter told me, "At least through all this, I learned to cry." The context for this statement began early on the morning following the crash. I had noticed him walk into the lobby with his wife's Japanese parents. They all appeared very stoic, not shedding one tear or showing emotion. Later, I noticed the man alone in the lobby staring out the front window. I went up to him and asked him if he would like to talk about it. Without looking at me, he merely nodded. We went to my room in the hotel. I asked for pictures of his wife and daughter. When I saw them, I began to cry. My daughter was the same age as his, and that was my projection and association that pushed my emotional button. We found ourselves crying on each other's shoulders for what seemed like hours. Before he left, he made the statement about learning to cry.

From these experiences I have concluded that people process trauma in different ways and at different rates. Studies have shown that couples process grief at different rates and are most commonly out of sync with each other in the process. The grief adjustment is no easier when each expects the other to be at the same stage.[24] Some enter at one stage, others at a different one. My experience suggests that these reactions are more cyclic than chronological. In this regard, I find the chart by Charles Figley very helpful for describing what the process of recovery looks like.[25] (See the chart "Stages of Recovery from Traumatic Events.") All of the descriptions and reactions noted above can be placed into his cyclic movement. What pleases me most about this chart is that it does not show regression to prior reactions as true regression but as part of the normal movement toward adjustment to the traumatic event. If all the above grief reactions can be thought of in the same vein, then it normalizes to a greater extent the common reactions of a traumatized person. These reactions become part of the scream that must take place in order to bring about true healing and adjustment.

Trauma has often been likened to throwing stones into a pond. The initial traumatic-stress reactions or grief responses can be thought of as the initial wake created by the stone. These are immediate waves and ripples that burst up after the stone has entered the water. What I will refer to as posttraumatic stress *reactions* are the subsequent ripples that move outward, forming increasingly larger circles but gradually diminishing in strength and size. These larger ripples are the reactions that last longer, and when they extend for more than six months after the initial trauma, are defined as posttraumatic stress *disorder*.

In short, a traumatized person has suffered an extreme blow from life or many blows that have had an accumulative effect over time. Initial reactions reveal some emotional responses of anger, depression, shock, or crying. There may be some behavior and cognitive changes like bargaining with God or denial that anything has happened and a wrestling to

Stages of Recovery from Traumatic Events

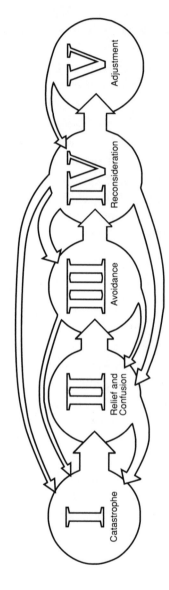

I Catastrophe

II Relief and Confusion

III Avoidance

IV Reconsideration

V Adjustment

(Thickness of arrows indicates approximate percentage of cohort shifts.)

find meaning. After six months or more, if the traumatized person has not completed his screaming work (working through the various stages or dramas), then screaming begins to emerge in different forms. There may be recollections of the trauma during sleep or from intruding thoughts. Some may experience flashbacks to such an extent that often smells, certain sights, or associations can trigger an instant replay of the trauma so that one believes the event is happening again. This traumatized person may be plagued by guilt, self-destructive behaviors, or certain startle reactions. She may also appear very numb to life. Things usually enjoyed are found wanting. Hobbies, recreations, and interests are no longer attractive or enjoyable. Avoidance of people may be characteristic.

The good news is that trauma is survivable! Though scar tissue forms during the healing process, the scarring itself is evidence of healing. Many who have survived have learned to live with their particular pains and hurts and have even used these to further the growth and development of their lives.

What these walking wounded have learned about what it takes to go on and become survivors is profound. They have an important message for us. We can learn much from their scars and pains. But we can also learn much from looking at those who have not done so well. Researchers have observed that there exist some important inhibitors to this screaming process. We want to scream, but for some reason the scream doesn't get all the way out . . . so our failure to scream merely retards our progress toward healing.

My limbs have not been torn from my body
So no one sees the pain I carry
My injury is deep, yet out of sight
Carefully guarded by a countenance so light
My affections have faded, lost all delight
Tenderness and touch has turned to fright
The love of my life has gone away
Saying she understands but just can't stay
So I carry on with a hole in my soul
God seems dead, survival is my goal
Though limbs are not severed from my body
The hole in my soul is more than I can ferry.
A Man in Pain

CHAPTER 3

Why We Don't Scream the Way We Should

While working on this book, I went to see the movie *The Doctor.* The doctor is played by William Hurt, an affluent, all-together, omnicompetent hospital physician. However, in the course of the movie he finds out that he has a cancerous growth on his throat. When the biopsy reveals that it is malignant, his world is turned upside down. The doctor now becomes the patient, and he doesn't like what he finds. The impersonal, dehumanized world of the cancer patient is thrust upon him. He doesn't know what to do with his feelings. His own medical knowledge and expertise are no help. Even his fellow physicians begin to function without him and talk around him. Even though his wife tries to understand what he is going through, he believes that she can't. In the midst of his confusion and anger he forms a relationship with a fellow radiation-therapy patient, a woman. This fellow griever introduces the doctor to the world of shared pain and coping, a world he had not known before. His own pain, anger, and lack of understanding begin to take on new meaning as he begins to listen to one who has been farther down the road of suffering. He begins to learn from the wounded, the walking wounded.

One of my favorite portions of the Bible deals with this concept. King Solomon was sort of an ancient Robin Leach. He made the life of being rich and famous a well-publicized news item throughout the ancient world. He did not withhold his hand from anything that claimed to be pleasurable and profitable. Yet when he sat down and seriously thought about the value of life, his conclusion was striking. He came to the conclusion that most of life is meaningless. However, from his acute observations of life he did see that amid the utter vanity of what we as humans do, some things are better than others. His conclusion illustrates a fundamental reality about life. We can learn more from our painful experiences than from our cocktail parties. Cocktail-party talk is an educational experience but not the kind we would want to base our life values on! Wise King Solomon observed:

> Better to go to the house of mourning
> Than to go to the house of feasting,
> For that is the end of all men;
> And the living will take it to heart. . . .
> The heart of the wise is in the house of mourning,
> But the heart of fools is in the house of mirth (Eccl. 7:2,4).

Solomon confirmed a reality that many professional therapists are admitting today. We need to listen to mourners. We need to listen to the victims, the traumatized, the diseased, and the ailing. Much is to be learned from them about what they have found helpful in surviving the blows of life. Somehow they go on, they learn to cope, they find meaning and hope where everyone else sees none. They are wounded, but they continue to walk. Henri Nouwen, a Catholic priest, has suggested that what qualifies one for the ministry today is being in touch with this pain. He wrote:

> The minister is called to recognize the sufferings of his time in his own heart and make the recognition the starting point of his service. Whether he tries to enter into a dislocated world, relate to a convulsive generation, or speak to a dying man, his service will not be perceived as authentic unless it comes from a heart wounded by the suffering about which he speaks.[1]

This is good advice for all the helping professions. Like William Hurt in *The Doctor*, until we experience our own hurt and discover the lessons in it, we are not in positions to help others. The true healers are the wounded healers who have learned from their pain the secrets of coping and surviving.

What we have learned from the walking wounded is not only what healthy coping looks like, a coping that leads to healing and meaningful reinvolvement in life, but also what hasn't helped. We all attempt to cope with the tragedies of life; however, some things work better than others. Therefore, before outlining what many sufferers have found helpful in surviving their screams, first it can be valuable to outline what might be characterized as dysfunctional coping. These are ways people attempt to move through their pain that are counterproductive. Researchers have observed some of these reactions, which over time only seem to keep the individual from adequately dealing with the sense of loss.

Dysfunctional Coping: Common Responses That Don't Work

Denial and Silence

A Vietnam veteran who shows up at the Los Angeles Airport is surprised by long-haired war protesters. They cry, "Baby killer" in response to seeing his neatly pressed uniform with all the military decorations. There's a cesspool of pain in the veteran's soul, but the initial "welcome" drives both his pain and verbal expression of it underground. He deals with Vietnam by not talking about it. On the other hand, I suspect that the true welcome we as a nation expressed toward the Gulf War veterans perhaps drove underground whatever expressions of pain they may have buried. It's a different set of circumstances, but for a Gulf War hero to express how painful the experience was may in the same way bring certain shame on him or her because the war was so antiseptic, with few casualties. No one should be hurting as a result!

I have written extensively on the Gulf War veterans' response in my book *Returning Home*. In that book I tried to detail some of the more toxic elements of the war that the press did not cover nightly. But what we have learned from the Vietnam experience is that denial and silence are not beneficial ways of coping. There does exist in some strange way the talking therapy. Naming and talking about our experiences, no matter how tragic, take much of their control and power away. Unfortunately, often the very people who should be supportive and should be facilitating this process feel very uncomfortable about hearing the details of our pain. One veteran's wife stated, "I didn't want to hear any more. It would totally destroy my image of what he was."[2]

Extended families also sometimes don't want to hear about the tragedies of their kids. It's easier to pretend that the experience didn't happen. One father told me that he couldn't bring himself to talk to his daughter about the rape she had experienced. His silence and pretending that everything would be fine if they didn't talk about it only added to the initial trauma. Talking about the experience with someone who is supportive and nonjudgmental is often the best initial therapy. Even Shakespeare acknowledged this good advice: "Give sorrow words: the grief that does not speak/ Whispers the o'er-fraught heart and bids it break."[3] Silence and denial, no matter how subtle, only further break the heart and bring no healing to the scream.

Blaming

As referred to in chapter 1, trauma raises the issue of injustice. Many things in life we bring upon ourselves. I make mistakes or don't really do as good a job as I should have done, and as a result, I receive a just recompense for my failure. But when traumatic events are thrust upon us unexpectedly, there is no real connection with my sense of fairness and justice. In the absence of such, the need to find blame is natural and normal. In the Delta 191 crash the blame was immediately placed on the air-traffic controllers, then on the meteorologists, then on the pilot, and finally on the FAA, which should have required all airports in the country to have Doppler radar (a superior radar technology capable of detecting wind shears). The need to find and place blame is foundational to the traumatic experience. However, as a long-term coping mechanism, blame can become counter-productive.

One of my friends who went through a divorce states openly that when he was denied entry into a graduate program, his immediate response was that it was his former wife's fault. So deep is our tendency to keep blame as a coping mechanism that even when things unrelated to the original trauma happen, they are used as evidence to justify the original blame. In the trauma of divorce, blaming the "ex" is normal, but ten years later, when not getting into graduate school is blamed on the "ex," this is evidence of a lack of healing.

The phenomenon of blaming can also be a problem to the family and friends of the victim. In rape cases victims often report that family, spouses, and friends blame the victim. Questions such as "Why weren't you more careful?" or "Are you sure you are telling the truth?" or "Did you enjoy it?" reflect this blaming-the-victim response. They feel that in some way the rape victim initiated or cooperated with the rapist and therefore is justifiably blamed. These responses only add to the extreme sense of humiliation and violation that the woman has already experienced. Researchers have noted that we all have the need to attribute blame in order to reduce our own amount of anxiety about the crime.[4] However, this blaming does not help. It brings no healing and only furthers the trauma for the victim.

As I reflect on one of the most famous stories from the life of Jesus, I am amazed by His modern insight into dealing with traumatic events. When a group of religious leaders brought a woman to Him and announced that she had been caught in the very act of intercourse with someone other than her husband, His response was intriguing. By the Jewish law she should have been stoned, so they asked Jesus what He thought should be done with her. Can you imagine what it must have been like for her to have been found in the most intimate of acts, dragged out of her house, and brought into the presence of a crowd of men? What amazes me about Jesus' response is that He never asked her how or why she had gotten herself in the situation. He didn't ask her, "Why were you sleeping with this man?" or "Are you a prostitute?" or "Didn't your father raise you right?" He merely accepted her as she was and then uttered His famous line "He who is without sin among you, let him throw a stone at her first" (John 8:7). After everyone left, He told her to "go and sin no more" (v.11). In one swift moment Jesus took the blame off her and placed it on everyone else. In her unjust, tragic moment Jesus met her where she was without blaming or condemning her.[5] Blaming is a useful transitional mechanism but a poor substitute for processes that can lead toward true healing.

Overprotection

When our lives have become shattered so that we see the world as a very hostile place, it changes the way we view all of our relationships. Phil Garcia remembers the time he was left for dead for a day and a half. He lay severely wounded in a grave surrounded by his dead buddies. The Vietcong were killing the survivors, so he stayed alive by covering himself with dead soldiers. In one day he saw 283 fellow army buddies killed. Twice married, he is now very much concerned about the effects of Vietnam on his five children. He readily rattles off a slew of statistics:

For every vet going through posttraumatic stress syndrome, it is estimated that two and three quarters of the immediate family is also victimized; 86 percent of runaways are children of Vietnam vets; the divorce ratio among Vietnam vets is 56 percent above the national rate.

Garcia explains, "You come back from the war, and you have these ways of behaving. . . . My wife and children became, in a sense, my platoon, and I was their sergeant. I would lead them through life."[6]

One way veterans have tried to cope with the realities they have faced is to protect their wives and children from harm. Having been harmed themselves, they do not want to see their loved ones harmed, so as a result, they overprotect their families and go to extremes to keep them from experiencing potential harm. One marine would not allow his wife to go out alone at night. Another veteran carefully scrutinized all his children's friends and "drilled" them for all the details about their whereabouts. Those having survived air crashes have serious reservations about their loved ones' flying. Fathers and husbands of rape victims sometimes become overly protective of their wives and daughters in an attempt to make up for their own perceived failure to protect their loved ones.[7] Again, these are natural and normal responses, but taken to the extreme, they become counterproductive in facilitating healing. No one can adequately protect loved ones from every potential harm. The same response has been seen in families in which one child has died or has a chronic illness.[8] In order to compensate for the dead child, the parent overprotects the remaining children. Sometimes parents form such a coalition with one child in an effort to protect the child that the other parent is excluded from the relationship. This does not bring about healing for the family but only adds to the trauma and loss for certain family members.

Research on children of Holocaust survivors has shown that overprotectiveness in all aspects of the parents' lives diminished the offspring's ability to establish outside relationships in general and marital and sexual relationships in particular. Many children raised with this overprotectiveness even dreaded becoming adults, and many feared having their own children. The fearful world of their parents was transmitted to the children![9]

As well motivated as overprotection often seems, its usefulness as a coping mechanism is not well regarded. It often causes the one being protected to be more drawn to danger in an attempt to break the tightly restricted boundaries that appear unreasonable, if not paranoid. Overprotection doesn't work and, in the final analysis, creates more problems than it solves. We can even overprotect ourselves. After the Delta crash many of the survivors felt that they could not fly again. Having seen the fire and rain, then unstrapping their seat belts and climbing out of the wreckage with only a few other survivors, is, for most, their worst nightmare. For many, flying again was unthinkable. This response is typical for those surviving air crashes. But we live in an airplane-dependent world today. Not to fly makes many things in our personal lives difficult. Trains are slower, can be real hassles, or don't go anywhere we need to go. Cars are even slower and, statistically, more dangerous than air travel. Yet the response to overprotect ourselves by never flying again is normal. Dr. Black was our volunteer psychiatrist. Soon after the August tragedy he began taking survivors back to the Dallas-Fort Worth Airport. He had Delta bring up an empty jet to an unused gate. He would go aboard with the survivor, then help him relax in his seat and get used to the sounds of jets taking off and landing again. All this was postcrash therapy while the jet was on the ground. When he felt that they were ready for their first flight, he would go along with them.

This strategy was just the old getting-back-on-the-horse-after-falling-off approach. With some it was very helpful. Others, like one of the surviving crew members, never flew again.

Overprotection also leads to another faulty strategy, that of avoidance.

Avoidance

Mary and John prided themselves on being the kind of parents who were involved in their kids' lives. Mary was active in the Parent-Teacher Association, and John never missed one of the kids' games. Their pride and joy were focused on their sixteen-year-old son. Handsome, popular, and a good student, he was also on the basketball team. He loved visiting his grandmother, even though he was a teenager. So when the opportunity came to spend a week in Florida with his grandmother, he jumped at the chance. After a week's visit, he was to return home to California. He had a layover in Dallas, a layover that would be permanent. John and Mary took the news with extreme difficulty. She said over and over, "It is a dream. I'll wake up in the morning and find James in his room." John was not very consoling. He promptly went back to work on Monday morning as if nothing had happened. Mary was furious. How could he do such a thing? She could barely function, and he was going back to work. This couple illustrates that most couples deal with trauma differently. John was avoiding dealing with his deeply felt pain and grief. His reaction is typical, but it becomes unhealthy over time. His initial solution to the death of his son was to keep busy. In fact, his number of work hours increased. He avoided coming home. Coming home represented having to face the reality of seeing an empty room and his son gone forever.

What makes this initial coping strategy so powerful is that it is often reinforced by friends, family, and sometimes work associates. It is also something that seems very simple to tell someone who has just received a terrible blow in his life. In an attempt to get his mind off what happened, we encourage him to go back to work or to work some extra hours. In effect, this keep-busy strategy only postpones proper healing by avoiding reality. Eventually, John will have to go home, face the empty bedroom, and begin to figure out what do to with his son's clothes and other personal effects. Though these are difficult times, they are part of the grieving process that must take place in order to deal adequately with the loss. Crosby and Jose have noted:

> By keeping busy we defend ourselves against the anxiety that arises when we are doing nothing. . . . Keeping busy enables us to put our mental-emotional energy into the task at hand, thus diverting thoughts and feelings away from death. As we struggle with our grief, we likely will have tasks to perform and worthwhile work to do. Keeping busy is, in itself, not wrong; the wrongness is in the fact that it turns into a dysfunctional strategy when it becomes the primary method of coping.[10]

Other common forms of avoidance are the increasing use of drugs and/or alcohol. Again, it is customary for psychiatrists to offer victims of traumatic events sedatives in order for them to sleep or mild antidepressants to help them get through the normal functions of the day. But when these become the primary means of functioning at all, they have become a problem. The drugs and alcohol have become means of not dealing with the loss or trauma. They are inhibiting the process rather than facilitating it. One specialist in disaster management told me somewhat jokingly, "After as many disasters as I have worked on, I don't go anywhere without my chaplain, my psychiatrist, and a bottle of Scotch—and not necessarily in that order." I know that his comment was in jest, but knowing what he had been through, I wondered if the accumulated stress of others had gotten to him and, rather than facing it directly, if he was merely avoiding it through alcohol.

Other examples of avoidance are taking trips, spending money, becoming promiscuous, and leaving departed loved ones' rooms intact. These are all understandable. Some divorcés, rather than dealing with the pain of the divorce, look for as many new partners as they can find. Numerous sexual encounters are subtle ways of numbing the pain of the valued loss. Others collect the departed's insurance money and go on a buying spree. Some make a shrine of the loved one's bedroom, keeping it just as he left it. Each of these may work temporarily to avoid dealing with the loss, but eventually they produce more long-term problems. Avoiding our own screams is avoiding reality, and avoiding reality is not healthy. We must face ourselves and what has happened and liberate our screams from the prison cells of our psyches. People who survive traumas are not avoiders; they are facers.

Inflexibility

George had no idea what was coming when he walked into his boss's office on Friday morning. As far as he knew, he had been doing a great job, had recently gotten several big contracts for the company, and was sort of the fair-haired rising star in the marketing area. He was shattered when his friend, the boss, said, "I'm afraid top management wants you out. . . . There's nothing I can do." In five minutes his world had gone from glorious to shattered. George was given a nice severance package and an office to work from until he found other work, but he couldn't get up enough courage to tell his wife. They had college payments to make; club memberships to keep up; and, of course, their house payment and some consumer debts. George figured that it wouldn't take long to find another job, so he would just keep his firing a secret. He got up every morning, went to the office, worked on his résumés, contacted headhunters (executive seek firms), and tried to find work. However, a job was not forthcoming. His financial package was all but gone, and he realized that it was time to level with his wife.

She was first shocked, then became angry, then grieved for him, and finally was very understanding. She quickly jumped to the aid of the family by saying that she would go to work. George did not want her to work but to be at home with the kids. Finally, in financial desperation she went to work. Six months later, they were both in counseling. She was working full-time, and he could find only a weekend part-time job that barely paid for the child-care expenses that allowed her to work. The problem? George was not able to face the trauma of unemployment with the needed flexibility.

Writers have documented that "sudden, unpredictable unemployment has devastating effects on individuals and families. It introduces a set of stressors into an individual's life situation and family system with no opportunity for preparation, either psychological or financial."[11] What happens in the trauma of unemployment and other traumas is that for the family to cope with the stressors, immediate changes have to be made. Changes necessitate differing role orientation, changing habits and schedules, and deciding who is going to do what. In this regard, one individual's coping mechanism may cause a second or third trauma to other members in the family. When Dad is laid off, other family members shift their habits since Dad is home more. A teenager may go to work, and the wife may work full-time rather than part-time or not at all. How everyone feels about these changes varies. The wife may enjoy the expanded role and having more say in the financial decisions in the family. Meanwhile, the husband may feel that he has been a failure, resenting the fact that his kids have to work. Therefore, the unemployment of one affects the whole family relationship and creates multiple stressors all at once. Families that are rigid have problems in making the necessary changes and cannot cope as effectively as those who are more flexible.

When trauma hits, it is normal to pull into a shell for a while to gain time and perspective. But eventually, reality must be faced, and this means making some necessary changes in order to survive. Individuals who are rigid and inflexible have a more difficult time adjusting to the trauma. It has been commonly reported that the survivors of the Holocaust were those who adapted quickly and were able to bring back some sense of control to their lives. Many of the aged and inflexible just lay down and died. Coping with trauma demands some flexibility.

Refusing Help

I am no psychotherapist, nor do I consider myself a Freudian. However, over the past few years I have been giving more serious consideration to the analysis of dreams. I was schooled in Freudian thought while majoring in psychology as an undergraduate student in college. Working on my master's degree in theology, I saw no place for dream analysis or any serious role for the human unconscious. Therefore, I rejected dream analysis outright as either unprovable from a research perspective or unbiblical from the perspective of my conservative, evangelical schooling. But discovering truth is always a serendipitous adventure. One never knows where a new insight into reality will come. One night while studying the prophet Daniel in the Bible (chapter 2), it dawned on me that Daniel, as the divine interpreter of the king of Babylon's dreams, had a particular method to dream analysis. In Daniel's interpretation Nebuchadnezzar was everything in his own dream. It seems that his whole dream contained elements of what was happening to him or what would happen. As I studied other dream interpreters like Joseph in the book of Genesis, the principle seemed to hold true (41:17–36). Could it be that what we dream about is our own life and what is going on in it? Maybe Freud had an element of truth after all. What this personal discovery has to say is one very important lesson I learned through one of my dreams.

Now don't get me wrong. I do not put much trust in my dreams or anyone else's. They are not authoritative for my life. I don't believe that I get divine guidance from my dreams as in biblical times. But I do want to recount for you one dream that led me to examine my own life in a particular area. I woke up one morning remembering my dream very vividly. As I reflected on its meaning, it began to reveal some amazing parallels with what was going on in my life at the time. Here was the dream.

I was in a crowd of people crossing over a deep hole. The hole had planks of plywood laid over it so that people could walk over the hole, the type seen around construction sites. As I approached the hole, several of the pieces of plywood began to break. As I saw them beginning to snap, I noticed in front of me a child who was about to place his foot on the plank. When he did, the wood broke completely, and the child fell into the very dark hole. I first stood in utter amazement. Then another child attempted to walk across another plank. It too broke, tumbling the second child into the same pit. With this I began to panic. I ran to the edge of the hole, hearing the children screaming but not being able to see them. I looked around for a rope or something to extend to them, but there was nothing. Then I tried to see if there was a way down for me to rescue them. There was none. Finally, in desperation I began to cry for help. Then I woke up.

As the imagery of the dream was still rattling around in my mind, I began to ask myself, *What in the world was this all about?* My heart was pounding. I had been there in the dream! So I applied my newfound theory of dream analysis. I am everything in the dream.

I am walking along, not anticipating harm to me or others. It is I in the dream. I see the planks covering a very deep hole. The planks are there to protect the passersby from harm and injury. So I asked, *What are the planks in my life?* Irony of ironies, as I evaluated my life at the moment, I was currently in the greatest upheaval of my forty-odd years. All the planks and supports of my life had become either broken, loosened, or removed. My career was up in the air, my income had significantly dropped, my wife had gone to work full-time, my kids were growing up and leaving the nest, and I was fighting a losing battle with mid-life midriff and associated problems in the mid-life experience. All the planks that I could count on were gone. Even the plank of God seemed distant or irrelevant. That part of the dream was very accurate.

But what about the kids falling into the abyss? Who were they? I let that question roll over in my mind for a while. Suddenly a flash of insight came. You are your dream. The child is me! My response to the upheaval in my life had not been the most mature. The horror, shock, and panic that I felt when I woke up were the feelings of a victimized child. I had fallen into the deep, dark pit when the planks of my life had become dysfunctional and broken. I was scared and screaming. The screaming was multiple. It's bad enough to be scared of your own screaming, but when it echoes back to you in the darkness, you do not know if it's your own or someone else's. It's a double dose of horror. I was in the pit as a scared child, screaming to be rescued.

Now move back to the top of the hole. Who was there? I was. I was the one looking down from above, concerned, trying to do what was right but not being able to find the means to do it. I was frustrated, angered, and panic-stricken to help but could find nothing that would work. That image was also very accurate. There were days when I would move from anger to depression. Some days I was so paralyzed by fear that I went into my office, shut the door, put my head on the desk, and literally couldn't function. Only periodic phone calls broke into my despair. I was looking for answers but not finding any. I felt the panic from my own pain but did not know what to do with it. I read books, I processed in my head, I argued with my wife and kids, I begged God to take my life. But nothing worked. Finally, I asked for help.

That's right. This whole dream-analysis thing is a long journey into my own experience to illustrate the point that the poorest way to deal with crisis is to try to solve everything ourselves. We can't save ourselves. We need outside help. When we are buried in a pit of despair and have tried everything to find some way out of it on our own, we need to dial 911, which may be in the person of a friend, the clergy, or a professional counselor, but we need to ask for help.

Now a word to male readers. We have a particular problem. It's not our thing to ask for help. Whether it is asking for directions when it is obvious to everyone in the car that we are lost, or when our marriage falls apart, or when we just carry around the silent shadow of grief from the pains in our lives, we need help. I wish somehow we could "demythologize" this thing called counseling in order to make it more attractive to men. Unfortunately, we have lost the important male turf where men have always processed their pain. All male bars, clubs, and organizations, where men were able to talk to other men apart from the presence of women, are gone today. Even the fishing or golf buddy has become uncommon for most men. Our pace of life and other priorities have taken away that arena of male processing. Today sharing pain has almost exclusively been dumped into the professional counselor's office, which is usually very costly financially or very uncomfortable for most men. Therefore, we usually have to be fairly desperate before we seek help. That's where I was. That's why my dream spoke to me. I needed to ask for help, and I did.

Deborah Tannen, in her best-selling book *You Just Don't Understand,* underscored why we men have such problems asking for help. From her research she found that men approach their relationships and communication styles within these relationships from the perspective of hierarchy. Referring to the differences encountered with her own husband, she wrote:

> Having done the research that led to this book, I now see that my husband was simply engaging the world in a way that many men do: as an individual in a hierarchical social order in which he was either one-up or one-down. In this world, conversations are negotiations in which people try to achieve and maintain the upper hand if they can, and protect themselves from others' attempts to put them down and push them around. Life, then, is a contest, a struggle to preserve independence and avoid failure. I, on the other hand (as a woman), was approaching the world as many women do: as an individual in a network of connections.... Life, then, is a community, a struggle to preserve intimacy and avoid isolation.[12]

Men have difficulty asking for help because they do not want to be placed in the inferior position of having to admit failure. To be in a therapist's office or to say to a friend that we are not doing well is to risk being in this inferior position. But we pay a heavy cost for this one-upmanship game when trying to deal with things like trauma and grief. The dysfunctional way of dealing with trauma is to pretend that nothing is wrong, bury the pain, and never ask for help. We would rather maintain the perceived hierarchical relationship in our heads than submit to the inferior position of asking for help.

Having considered the ways that do not bring about healing and recovery, we are now in a better position to look at what the wounded have taught us about surviving trauma. These are the insights gained from the wounded warriors and the harmed heroines. It is truth born in pain.

Sweet are the uses of adversity
Which, like the toad, ugly and venomous,
Wears yet a precious jewel in his head.
                              William Shakespeare
                              As You Like It[1]

Pain provides an opportunity for heroism;
The opportunity is seized with surprising frequency.
                              C. S. Lewis[2]

CHAPTER 4

What We Have Learned from the Screams of Others

ecovery is in. Go into any bookstore today and look at the self-help section. Recovery books fill the shelves—recovery from alcoholism or from being a child of an alcoholic; recovery from eating disorders, sexual addictions, physical abuse; recovery from codependency, being a workaholic, or a church addict. It's all there. I don't mean in any way to minimize the need for this self-help literature. However, at times it seems that it has gotten a little out of hand. I fully expect to see recovery titles for pet-aholics, Oprah-holism, and how to recover from being a man who loves too little, married to a woman who loves too much because her sister was anorexic and her mother was an adult child of an obsessive-compulsive gardener! Of course, each of these new "addictions" has some kind of step program associated with its recovery process. Adapted from the original AA program of 12 steps, each has its unique variation on a theme.

I have said all this to suggest that posttraumatic-stress disorder is in a different category when it comes to recovery. I don't believe there is any five-, ten-, or twelve-step program to make pain go away or to bring about quick recovery. Although many of the concepts in the step programs have many helpful elements, they may or may not be directly related to dealing with the extreme traumas that many people face today. What I will relate in this section is what sufferers of extremely traumatic events have found helpful while enduring the initial trauma and during the recovery period. Julius Segal, a psychologist with over thirty years' experience in dealing with prisoners of war, hostages, and Holocaust survivors, has observed:

> Crises and trauma are facts of life, and there are precious lessons to be learned from those who have been challenged to the very limit—and triumphed. I am talking about the real thing—surviving catastrophic events—and not about handling the everyday irritants of life.[3]

What Dr. Segal is talking about is something of a different order when it comes to coping. Here there are no step programs, though some of the principles may be helpful for some. Here are no quick fixes, or techniques, or relaxation or meditation devices. Suggested here are merely some broad, overarching principles or strategies for learning to live with what has happened in the worst-case scenarios of life. These strategies should encourage us that despite the severity of traumatic events, they can be survived. The keys to this survival lie in developing some life strategies. Again, Segal has noted:

For over three decades, I have studied victims of overwhelming stress—concentration camp survivors, POWs liberated from years of captivity, terrorized hostages. Repeatedly, I have been inspired by the countless cases that run counter to "expert" predictions. Instead of a pattern of deficit and defeat, there is one of coping and conquest. Indeed, rather than being devastated by their suffering, many survivors have actually used the experience to enrich their lives. . . . Until recently, the human capacity for conquering life crises appears to have been one of psychology's best-kept secrets. Human beings have a magnificent ability to rebuild shattered lives, careers, and families, even as they wrestle with the bitterest of memories.[4]

One of these courageous conquerors is Barbara. In a period of ten years she has had more than her share of traumatic events. By all professional opinions she should be falling apart. Instead, she is still giving to others and remaining hopeful about her own good and the goodness of God. During this period she lost her mother through brain cancer, and her husband had two heart attacks, the second of which left him paralyzed and unable to speak. Her son also had a malignant brain tumor. Finally, Barbara herself was diagnosed with cancer in both lungs. When asked, "What keeps you going?" she replied, "The Lord, my friends and family, and just thinking it could be worse." How can this be? From where does such a response come? Maybe Barbara and a host of others have learned something we need to learn. How have they been able to cope and heal from such radical exposure to trauma?

The Human-Touch Factor

I used to have a sign over my desk with an inscribed motto, which formed a semicircle around a cute turtle. The motto read, "Behold the turtle, who never makes progress until he sticks his neck out." Turtlology has much in common with human nature. The turtle has to stick its neck out in order to make progress, but it also has enough sense to know when impending danger is about to strike and pulls into his shell. Our instinctive response to trauma is the same psychologically. When we have become bruised and beaten by the blows of life, we pull in, hide, and hope the danger lying outside will eventually go away. All this takes place in the deep recesses of our human psyches. But sometimes the pain is too great and the fear too paralyzing for us to be able to stick our necks out again in order to make forward progress. So we stay in our protective mental shells. One Vietnam nurse recounted her "shell-shock" experience when she was twenty-two. She recalled:

> Blood and flesh were so much a part of our lives. You never forget that smell. In order to handle the situation you walled yourself in, you insulated yourself against the pain you wanted to feel, the pain the enlisted soldiers were feeling. You didn't want to come home crazy. You wanted to protect your psyche, so you put it in a special little closet, closed the door and didn't let yourself feel it anymore.[5]

When this happens, it takes someone else to reach into our closeted psyches and pull out our frightened heads. We need the human touch of others to survive. Whether it is the actual physical touch or merely keeping in touch through verbal communication, we cannot be left in our pain alone. The rugged individualist does not seem to work in this field. For victims to become survivors, the human connection must take place and take place almost immediately.

When the Air Florida flight crashed into the Potomac

River after leaving National Airport, most of the passengers were immediately submerged in the dark, icy-cold waters. Very few passengers escaped the rapid descent into the depths of the Potomac. Within hours the navy Seals were on the scene, doing their well-rehearsed diving routine. Their task was to bring up the bodies of the passengers still trapped in the coffin of the jetliner. Navy Seals are thought of in the military establishment as the finest, the toughest, and the best trained of the special forces. But in the dark hours and early morning of the next day chaplains were placed in tents on the banks of the river. The tough Seals would take turns coming up from their dives and unloading on the chaplains about what they were seeing and experiencing. One of the navy Sprint team members shared what was happening with the divers: "In the darkness of the river and not being able to see more than one foot in front of your face, suddenly there would be a body right in front of you. It was freaky, eerie." These tough, well-trained special elite of the navy were freaking out. As well trained as they were, they were still human, with wives, sons, and daughters of their own. They needed a human touch. When they came up, the chaplains put their arms around them, offered them coffee, and got them to talk about what they had seen. In the midst of the traumas these divers needed to feel human again. They needed to talk. They needed to be comforted. The touch was both physical and verbal, but the healing was at a psychological level.[6]

The human-touch factor was the primary principle active in the American POW communication system in Vietnam. Senior officers and long-timers in the Hanoi Hilton took amazing risks and used incredible "Yankee ingenuity" in order to keep alive the human-touch factor among the prisoners.

Capt. Eugene McDaniel (U.S. Navy) revealed that this human-touch factor was the lifeline to survival. He wrote:

> In all of this, we continued to communicate. When the VC put us out in the gardens to work, sometimes this garden would be behind a building we had not been able to communicate with, so we pounded out the code in the clumps of dirt with our shovels. The VC, of course, were not shrewd enough to catch on. Another tack was the following: When a guard was next to me, I would look at him and direct a question at him in English, a question a guy in the building could hear. The guard . . . would look at me queerly, not comprehending and not realizing that I was communicating with the man inside. We pounded out the code on our walls, taking polls as to the most beautiful movie star . . . the athlete of the century and the man of the century. So we entertained ourselves as best we could.[7]

One of my classmates in graduate school had been a POW for seven years. One of his first experiences was being placed in a dark box for days on end. He related to me that in that darkness and insanity he would hear in English, "Have a nice day, Jerry." He said he could live for weeks on that one statement. Knowing that another American had risked his life in order to communicate with him was just enough human touch to keep on living. It was a reminder that somewhere there was still an ounce of sanity left in the world. All was not bleak.

I don't believe we fully realize how dependent we are on the human connections that constantly reaffirm our own humanness. What happens in traumatic events is that we feel victimized to such an extent that we can't get our heads back out of our shells. Like the POW who is so traumatized that his natural tendency is to lie down and die, the key to his survival lies with those who constantly break through the emotional and physical barriers to touch the person. For those having been traumatized, they must realize the importance of opening to those reaching out.

The above illustrations are rather extreme, but all trauma is felt with extreme intensity. Pain is pain, and it is always experienced individually with a unique sense of intensity. I agree with C. S. Lewis, the Oxford scholar, that there is not such a thing as the sum of suffering that is experienced by one person. One million sufferers who suffer the same pain do not add more pain to the one experiencing his own pain.[8] We each bear our own pain, even though it will be revealed in the next chapter that there does exist a vicarious sense of corporate pain that one can absorb. But for our purposes here, whatever the pain we bear as the result of traumatic events, when we pull into our shell, we are refusing to scream. This refusal is tantamount to saying that we will not survive. To survive is to open to the human touch, which must come from without. What is it about this human connection that brings about healing and recovery? The answer lies in some of the most profound research on the value of social supports.

As we look back on the Vietnam era and how we treated our soldiers, one thing has become certain. We blew it! We put new recruits into already cohesive units. When the tour of duty was over, we sent him or her home alone! Even the wounded were moved to the rear immediately, never to see their buddies again. Soldiers woke up in rear hospitals without legs or arms or badly mutilated, no longer in their uniforms but in hospital gowns, stripped of identity, dignity, and continuity with the only other guys who knew what had happened. It's no wonder that our veterans have not done

well. The value of immediate social support became apparent
to me when I attended the International Congress on War-
time Stress, hosted by the Israelis.

At the conference the Israelis shared what they had
learned from their experience in the Lebanon war, as con-
trasted with their other wars, in which they felt major mistakes were made in treating psychological casualties. First,
they assigned a mental-health officer to every combat unit.
This officer's duty was to process the feelings of the soldiers
as soon as the bullets stopped flying. This was first-echelon
mental-health care.[9] When there was a medical casualty, the
attempt was made to keep him at the front as long as possible. This was not a medical decision but a mental-health decision. It was reasoned that the only individuals who could
really understand what had happened in that particular
firefight were the other unit members who were there. When
a wounded soldier was evacuated, his uniform was left on. In
the hospital he was to wake up from surgery still in his uniform. By our American medical standards this sounds sense-
less, if not medically unsound. However, the Israelis have put
a priority on saving the human spirit as much as the body.
When soldiers go home, tributes are published in newspapers. Families and relatives buy space in the papers to honor
their heroes! Then attempts are made to involve the entire
family in postwar counseling after the veteran comes home.
The point of all this effort is that the Israelis have recognized
that without the social-support mechanism in place, survival
of the psychological trauma is difficult.[10] As we study our own
veterans, we learn that the ones who have faired better than
most have both left and returned to strong social supports:

> One suspects that the most significant influence on the veter-
> an's sense of himself, the quality of his life before the war, and

on his perception of combat as a duty, an opportunity to prove himself, or an escape from home, is his family. . . . Five of ten combat veterans we have seen [in their book] who did not develop post-traumatic stress disorders came from warm, supportive families. . . . What this suggests is that family background, in interaction with many other factors, can operate to protect veterans from stress disorders following combat.[11]

Having a supportive spouse and having a larger support system like a church or synagogue have also proved critical to reduced levels of PTSD.[12] Psychologist James Pennebaker reported the results of more than two thousand people who had suffered trauma, including physical abuse, rape, or the death of a loved one. Survivors were healthier, he found, if they managed to confide in someone about the event. Those who hadn't discussed their experiences developed more illnesses of various sorts—from headaches to lung disease.[13] Even the perception that social support and help are available has been proved to diminish initial catastrophic stress.[14]

A caring, supportive, understanding community is essential in providing the human-touch factor. Once we finally begin to scream, we need people who are not afraid of the screams but who can provide the needed shoulder to cry on. Without such, our screams go unheeded or misunderstood, and so we bury them and continue to bleed to death on the inside.

Victims who have people in their lives who can understand their pain are, then, in a much safer position to take the risk to stick their heads out and make forward progress. But once the head is out, there are some other things the traumatized can do. Another factor related to making further progress and bringing about healing is that of taking up the sword. To survive, we must fight for our own healing.

Taking Up the Sword: Regaining Control

I have a good friend who is a psychologist, so I get a lot of free advice! On one occasion as we were psychologizing about life, I asked him, "What in your opinion is the most common denominator in most of the problem people you see?" I thought it was a good question, but I wasn't prepared for his answer. Without much thought he blurted, "Control issues."

That's right. Most of our difficulty in managing and adapting to life's constantly changing environment centers on either too much control or not enough control. Sometimes women view men as into control and having to control everything; therefore, when men are out of control, they fall apart. There is probably some truth to this; however, the other extreme is just as destructive and unproductive. Recovery from trauma does not lie in merely lying down and doing nothing because one feels out of control. This is not where mental health or recovery lies either, especially when it comes to dealing with and recovering from severe crises in our lives. As seen in chapter 1, the dynamics of trauma cause us to lose all control when our world gets shattered. Now both the world and where we fit into it are totally and seemingly irreversibly out of control. As human beings made in the image of God, we have been given a certain stewardship of our environment (see Gen. 1:26). We have the deep-seated need to rule the environment of our lives. The divine design is to rule it with wisdom, benevolence, and equity. However, as fallible humans we mess up the design. Obsessive-compulsives rule too much; dysfunctionals rule too little. Trauma makes the best people dysfunctional for a while. But when we begin to come out of our shells through supportive care, we need to regain some of the lost control. We must take up the sword and do some dragon killing.

In psycho-jargon, this principle is called reestablishing the locus of control. For our own mental maintenance we need a place or sphere that we can control. We can't control everything, but we need to regain the control of something. In regaining the smallest areas of control, we can begin to rebuild our shattered identity and world.

When General Dozier, the American NATO Army commander in Italy, was taken captive by the Italian Red Guard, he knew he had to regain some sense of control. This principle is now actively taught in our military-survival schools. But what could he do? He was blindfolded and handcuffed to his bed, with a radio headset over his ears, blaring rock music for most of his days and nights. The only thing that interrupted this boredom was when his captors would bring him out for communist brainwashing. His world had become severely limited to mere existence, without even the human touch that the POWs had in Hanoi. General Dozier was totally isolated except for the few hours every day when his captors tried to convert him. He realized that he had to take up the sword. In his shattered world he could still take the mental offensive. In his mind he boned up all day for his interrogation time, as if he were studying for a final exam in college. He said that he even began to look forward to this one human connection every day when he could at least dialogue with his captors. He took the position of trying to sell them on the merits of democracy and capitalism, never capitulating to their communist rhetoric. After several days he asked if he could begin an exercise program. They relented and allowed him to do push-ups and to run in place. This was another sphere of control for him. Every day he tried to beat his record from the day before. He was out of control but maintaining some control. After many days General Dozier was rescued.[15]

One of the Marine sergeants assigned to the embassy in Tehran had another way of maintaining a sense of control when out of control. As a Hispanic fluent in Spanish, when confined to one small room as a hostage for the 444 days of captivity, he found great delight in putting one over on his captors. He wrote in Spanish certain phrases on the walls of his room. When his non-Spanish-speaking captors asked him what it said, he told them, "It says, 'Allah be praised.'" The Iranian captors were so impressed that they brought in photographers to take pictures of the inscriptions, which were released to Western newspapers. To the Spanish-speaking world it was a joke on the Iranians. In Spanish the inscription read, "Khomeini is an [expletive deleted]!" It was this semper fi' marine's way of gaining control in an impossible situation.[16]

When our everyday lives are interrupted by traumatic stressors that disconnect us from the things we have learned to take for granted, we need to take up the sword. Finding something that we *can* do every day is critical to our survival. For Ambassador Bruce Laingren of the U.S. embassy in Iran it was as simple as shaving every day. He said, "It helped preserve my fading self-image."[17] The only thing that removes the feelings of helplessness that the traumatic stressors bring is taking up the sword.

In chapter 3 I alluded to a period in my life when I perceived my life falling apart, with all the planks supporting me being broken and removed. During that time I often sat in my office immobilized by fear, anger, and frustration. During that time I conceived the idea of a book about how uneasy being a man is in today's society. During my bouts with depression I began to write, muse, and interact with other men to see if they ever felt the same things. I remember taking what I considered a gigantic risk for me. I went to lunch with another man who had worked for the same organization I was currently working for. I didn't know him very well. I didn't know if I could trust him. I knew that he knew everybody who was causing problems in my life at the time. Talking to him could get me fired if it ever reached certain people. But I was taking the sword in hand. I was doing something about what I was feeling. We went to lunch, and during that time I said, "I'm going to lay everything out before you that I'm feeling. By the end you tell me whether you think I'm crazy." I was serious. I needed help. But I knew that help wasn't going to come from being cloistered in my office every day. I needed to *do* something. I needed some sense of control over my life again. This was the first attempt. By the end of lunch my newfound partner smiled and said, "Your experience is the same I had when I worked there. Personally, I wouldn't trust my life with any of the men in leadership there."

Wow, that was all I needed. A brother in arms. In one lunch I had accomplished two things: the first survival principle, human touch, and the second, taking up the sword. He hadn't thought I was crazy. He agreed and went further than where I was in my own life. He also modeled in front of me that what I was going through was survivable. I appreciate this friend for helping me take up the sword.

You see, without regaining some sense of control, we become very vulnerable to the feelings of complete impotence. I saw myself as powerless, and this is not healthy for even normal existence. We must take charge of some area of our life and slay the mental and psycho-dragons that convince us that there is nothing we can do. By the way, the book I wrote during that time, *Uneasy Manhood*, is now a well-selling (by faith) volume that has opened up many new career opportunities. My writing career was born during the time of my greatest trial. It gave me a sense of control I needed. It also provided a crucial temporary meaning for the pain I felt, which allowed me to survive the crisis. Meaning and purpose are critical to survival. This is another important principle we have learned by listening to the wounds of others. In order to survive, we must find some purpose for the pain.

Finding Purpose in Our Pain: Giving Meaning to the Meaningless

Remember Barbara? When asked how she could cope with so many traumas during the span of ten years, she replied, "The Lord." She went on to recount how her faith in the Lord had given her the conviction that there was some meaning in the multiple tragedies, even though she did not know what the specific meaning was. She said, "I know the Lord will use this somehow for my good and for His glory." Is this pious God-talk? Many skeptics and mental-health professionals of the past may have thought so but no more. It is increasingly recognized that in order to survive difficult times and tragic events, the individual must find some purpose or significance in what he is experiencing.

In one of my Society for Traumatic-Stress Studies conferences I was sitting in a workshop, listening to a presenter develop this concept. I was somewhat fascinated and excited that a mental-health professional was so openly discussing the merits of meaning in regard to traumatic stress. I was educated in the era when spiritual or theological issues were never seen as relevant to the field of mental health or, worse, were considered a detriment to it. So here I was, surrounded by a group of psychiatrists, psychologists, and other mental-health workers, seeing all sorts of nodding that the presenter was on target. I couldn't resist any longer. I had to raise my hand and ask a question. When acknowledged, I commented, "It seems to me that if what you are saying is true, that survivability is related to finding meaning, then you are outside your field. Isn't the subject of meaning and purpose more in the field of philosophy, theology, or religion?" I was expecting the negative reaction I had encountered back in my undergraduate years when my professors were anything but believers in ultimate purposes or life meaning. To my surprise, the presenter looked at my Air Force uniform, noticed the cross above my ribbons, and said, "You are right. I am outside my field. That's why we need people like you in this association!"

God does work in strange ways. It seems to me that mental-health professions have sort of backed themselves into the importance of meaning by their own research methodology. As they have diligently studied the lives of the traumatized and how they have survived and learned to cope, they have found a truth that sometimes their own profession has not wanted to admit. These are religious questions ... issues of faith, struggles of the soul, questions that get at why we are here and what life is all about and what is really important. Psychology or medicine does not prepare one for these questions. Sometimes even our churches and seminaries don't either. But they are important, fundamental issues when facing life-threatening situations and surviving their aftermath. To survive requires seeing some meaning in the pain.

This search for meaning will be discussed in further detail in the next chapter, in which many other theological issues will be raised. However, for the purposes of this chapter it is important to note that the search for meaning is one of the most foundational responses during the posttrauma period. It is therefore very important to see that this search for meaning must begin to find some temporary meaning that can allow the victim to survive. Even in the most tragic situations if some meaning can be found, then our coping ability has become greatly enlarged. In the insanity of Nazi Germany the German scientists turned their scientific inquiry into the horror of human experimentation. They were fascinated in studying how cold temperatures humans could withstand or what different types of operations could be done on humans without anesthesia. In one experiment they had a group of Jewish prisoners dig holes all day long and then at the end of the day fill in the holes. They had another group of prisoners dig the deep communal graves into which their own fellow Jews were then machine-gunned to death. The survival rates of those doing the digging for their own dead were far higher than those doing the meaningless work of mere digging and filling.

We are purposeful creatures. We need to see meaning and purpose in what happens in our lives. When there is none, we grope for it. Even our search for meaning, in some inextricable way, gives us some meaning. Researchers note that the loss of a child so strikes at the heart of our rational world assumption that the search for meaning becomes specifically exaggerated for the parents:

An aspect of the parental experience that is frequently overlooked is the parents' "search for meaning" . . . in which the parents urgently tried to make sense out of the tragedy. This search would take various forms such as seeking out some personal agency to be blamed for the disease or placing it within the realm of God's will. The loss of any loved one may stimulate such a quest for meaning. However, the violation of the natural order in the child's predeceasing the parent cries out for the assignment of meaning to an otherwise meaningless event. Several writers have pointed out that the search for meaning is an essential part of the grief work of bereaved parents in coming to some resolutions of their child's death.[18]

Are these searches for meaning successful? Sometimes they are; sometimes they may be prolonged in coming. When they are successful, bereaved parents note such positive effects as "having a stronger faith, or being more compassionate, or being more caring toward others or being able to live life more fully because of an increased awareness of the preciousness and frailty of life."[19] For these, seeing even the limited meaning of personal growth or valuing life more preciously offers a "reason" for the severity of the trauma of losing a child.

Whether or not we like it, whether or not we realize it, the personal meaning we attach to our crisis gives us the necessary rationale to go on. This is why the Vietnam veteran has had such difficulty in working through the aftereffects of war. The search for meaning has been found wanting. In the lack of meaning the veteran's coping abilities and progress toward healing have been greatly frustrated. Hendin and Haas have detailed this dilemma:

Vietnam veterans certainly share this difficulty [difficulty in finding a personal meaning]. Their sense of a war fought without the total commitment of the government or the full support of the American people, their lack of clear understanding of the military or political objective of the war, and their inability at times simply to identify the enemy, all helped persuade them that there was something casual and unnecessary about the killing and dying in Vietnam. Their attempt to come to terms with the personal meanings of their combat experiences is confounded by their socially shared sense of suspicion and dislocation from a country that to many seemed indifferent about their lives.[20]

For the veteran, finding personal meaning in a meaningless war has been difficult. Survivors have had to find meaning in other areas, since the national meaning was so purposeless. Veterans who have faired better than others have shared how many of the things learned in Vietnam have been used to further their own growth and professional development. One army ranger put his learned survival skills to good use and founded a camp for boys where these skills were given a benevolent twist. After a marine medic finished his tour of duty, he went to college and medical school. The interest created by an insane war provided the key to his postwar goals and career. Today he is a practicing suburban physician who still maintains a close affinity to other veterans and their continuing medical problems.

Often the meaning needed to provide the necessary coping resources are not all that sophisticated. One best-selling author told the story of visiting his mother as a middle-aged adult and finding a crumpled picture of himself as a baby. When he asked his mother why the photo was in such poor condition, she replied with a story that had never been revealed to him about his father, who had died shortly after the author's birth. His mother explained that his father had contracted polio shortly after the birth of his son. During this time he was confined to an iron lung, which literally breathed for him. What gave the writer's father a purpose to live every day was the photo of his son fastened to his iron lung, jammed between the metal knobs of the life-support cylinder. Thus, the crumpled condition of the baby photo.[21] Who knows how this small but significant purpose for living contained in one photo of a father's son gave this victimized man a few more days and months of life?

Sometimes the things that keep us going and give us meaning to survive are the most mundane things. Gerta Weissman looked back forty years to her experience as an inmate of Nazi concentration camps. She stated:

> You know, when people ask me, "Why did you go on?" there is only one picture that comes to mind. That moment was when once I stood at the window of the first camp I was in and asked myself probably the most important question of my life. I asked if, by some miraculous power, one wish could be granted to me, what would it be? . . . And then, with almost crystal clarity, the picture came to my mind. And what I saw was a picture at home—my father smoking his pipe, my mother working at her needlepoint, my brother and I doing our homework. And I remember thinking, my God, it was just a boring evening at home. I had known countless evenings like that. And I knew that this picture would be, if I could help it, the driving force to my survival.[22]

When my kids get bored, I tell them this story. Their boredom (the worst American teen nightmare) may sometime be the key to their survival!

It is true that what allows the wounded to keep going is finding some controlling meaning or purpose. Pain is tolerable when we can connect it with some meaning, even a temporary meaning. Many of the concentration-camp survivors like Gerta Weissman had their families' or spouses' mental portraits, which gave them reasons for existence during incredible duress, only to find, once the war was over, that their reasons for living were gone. However, the reasons were sufficient to get them through the immediate ordeal. The issue of ultimate meaning and why this also plays an important role in survivorship will await the next chapter. Segal has stated, "To fill the void left by our losses, it is not necessary . . . for us to discover that elusive, ultimate, cosmic meaning of life. We need only find meaning in what we do today, tonight."[23] I would agree with Segal that we need this immediate meaning in order to survive the trials of today. However, I believe a growing body of research would confirm that we as humans also need some ultimate meaning for our pain when the temporary meanings have failed us. To survive, we need to find some purpose in the pain, make some immediate sense of the suffering. Survivors find this meaning and purpose in even the smallest hope. But once the sword has been taken in hand and some meaning found, it is time to begin slaying the dragon of guilt.

Slaying the Dragon of Guilt: Facing the Feelings of Failure

When United flight 232 careened over and over, throwing airplane pieces and people into the surrounding cornfields at the Sioux City Airport, the fire fighters were ready and waiting on the tarmac. Their first responsibility was to put the fire out, since that was their job. But once on the scene, where they found people crying out, they faced many instant decisions of whether to help the screaming people or put the fire out so that others still inside the plane might live. Several of the fire fighters for weeks afterward fought the dragon of guilt. Did they do the right thing? Should they have helped the screaming woman? Would that child have lived if they had stopped to take some time with him?—questions that drive everyday, normal people crazy. A chaplain at the scene recorded:

> A firefighter is feeling guilty because the new tanker truck would not work properly. After having it malfunction in the field, he drove it back to the shop where it worked perfectly. He drove it back to the field where it again malfunctioned. . . . He is pouring down coffee and says he can see the nightmares coming. . . . Other firefighters reassure him that it was indeed the equipment's fault and not his.[24]

Feeling guilty for not being able to do enough or for possibly not doing the right thing and feeling responsible for the loss of others—these are the dragons that traumatic events bring forth. They are not easily slain, but the survivors learn to take the sword in hand and begin the process of jabbing at them. Rape victims often blame themselves for not being smarter or more careful. Even their families, boyfriends, and husbands feel a particular sense of guilt for not adequately protecting the victim. Burge has observed:

> Often parents or mates of rape victims experience considerable guilt and a sense of responsibility for the rape. . . . For example, a family fight may send an adolescent female out of the house in a rage. If she is subsequently raped, while away from home and emotionally distraught, her parents may experience a frenzy of self-blame, feeling responsible for their daughter's vulnerable state. . . . Following a rape, parents and

husbands of victims may feel that they have failed in their duties as protectors.[25]

Feeling the pain of guilt for what one should have done can be devastating for many. However, survivors learn that to overcome these normal feelings, they have to face their perceived failure, find self-forgiveness, and accept the reality that they are human. The fire fighter in Sioux City must realize that no one could have done everything that needed to be done. We are self-limited by time and space and prior training. Fire fighters know that their first job is to put out the fire to save lives. To feel guilty for those who may have died while the flames were being extinguished is normal but not rational. Self-forgiveness must be granted and perhaps a recognition gained that the actions taken *did* save many additional lives.

Pilots who were shot down in Vietnam have wrestled with their own sense of failure. Did they do the right thing, did they "screw up," or could they somehow have evaded that incoming missile? As recently as Desert Storm I have also heard the same moralizing over friendly fire. The families of those killed by friendly American fire have their own unique grief to bear. But what about the A-10 pilot who replays the mission over and over in his mind? How could he have made the mistake? The image on his heads-up display looked like an Iraqi tank, but it wasn't. Consequently, American lives are on his hands. This individual must find some room in his omnicompetent Tactical Air Command-trained, fighter-pilot self-image to allow for failure. He needs to see that he did the best he could in the circumstances and that he made a mistake, which is only human. He must adjust his self-posture, learn from the experience, cut himself some slack, and kill the dragon of self-blame.

For those who have been more actively involved in things they consider wrong, the problem is more complicated. The earlier illustration of Corporal Smith is one such person. At the time he did what every soldier in his squad did. But twenty years later he can't tolerate the thought that he willingly did such horrible acts. Killing and maiming "gooks" and fragging (killing one's own) officers were a part of the Vietnam motif. But now it doesn't fit reality. What Corporal Smith feels is not an irrational guilt for not doing enough but perhaps a true moral guilt based on a deep-seated conscience of right and wrong, which no military establishment, psychiatrist, or alcohol can ever dull. The moral implications of this kind of guilt will be discussed further in the next chapter on theological issues in trauma. But for the moment Corporal Smith has a more tenacious beast to kill. He needs forgiveness that is more than self-forgiveness, a mere acceptance of human frailty and finiteness. He needs forgiveness from outside himself.

If our natural tendency to feel guilty in response to traumatic events is not checked and the dragon slain, our ability to recover is greatly inhibited. Survivors begin to say to themselves, *If I have failed, I'm human. If I did all I could do, then I'm not going to kick myself around for not doing the impossible.* The reason we hang on to the demon of guilt may be that it provides a sense of meaning or an explanation that we still need. It reinforces our belief in a just and fair world and therefore plays a more important role than just making us take responsibility for something out of our control. Sometimes the guilt trip will be maintained by others who are still struggling with their own meaning and purpose for the event. It is easier to find meaning in blaming the victim (especially in rape) than to accept that there was no apparent reason for the tragedy and thus no real meaning. We place guilt on those who have found themselves in situations or traumas that we have no explanation for. At least placing blame resolves in an inappropriate way the meaning question.

It is interesting to note that when, instead of blame, there is welcome acceptance, the recovery process is greatly enhanced. Have you noticed the apparent difference between the average Vietnam veteran and the POWs? Our POWs were tortured, were denied basic necessities, were not allowed free communication with other prisoners, and were not given needed medical attention. The time lost from their lives was profound. They came home to grown kids or kids they had never seen. For them too the entire culture had changed. But it is apparent by most authorities that their recovery has been better than that of the other veterans.[26] Why? Because in 1973 we needed heroes. We needed to salvage something of meaning from the Vietnam experience. Our culture welcomed the POWs in the same fashion that the Desert Stormers were welcomed home. They were given parades, receptions, and presidential recognition. Not so for the average grunt. He continued to bear his pain alone, unrecognized and blamed for being a part of a crazy war.

Victims need the welcoming reception by others in order to slay this dragon. They feel enough guilt within themselves naturally. They do not need more from their friends, relatives, or society. But there is still one more thing that survivors do to bring about further healing.

Helping Others Pick Up the Sword: Helping Yourself by Helping Others

Military commanders are not exactly the best grief counselors. The role almost seems inconsistent with their office and rank. However, as more research on the field of traumatic stress becomes available, one fact is beginning to stand out. There exists a very important phenomenon called grief leadership, which places extreme importance on leaders' openly acknowledging their own pain during difficult times.[27] Basically, the concept involves seeing a certain hierarchy to the grief process. Freedom to grieve or feel what an individual is feeling must come from without and must come from someone perceived to be in a higher position. Permission to grieve then descends downward throughout an organization or family, beginning at the top levels. What this means is that one of the best ways to deal with traumatic stressors is to help others work through their own feelings of grief. In the military organization it means that chaplains and commanders can take the lead by openly revealing their own dismay and sense of loss at tragic events. Chaplain Clapper again noted the grief leadership displayed in himself and his own commander. Following the United Airlines crash, his Air National Guard unit was assigned much of the cleanup and continuing assistance in body identification. He wrote:

> Today is the day that the bodies will be removed from the crash site. I roam from team to team. At one point, about 100 of the ANG personnel are on the runway milling around watching 2 bodies being bagged. I stand up in the back of a pick-up truck and ask all those present to stop for a moment of prayer. There is no resistance to this suggestion and I read the 23rd Psalm in an admittedly cracking voice and say a short prayer. A few days later one of our troops came up to me and said, "Say, you almost lost it out there the other day." . . . It struck me later that there are many different ways of being a professional. Maybe the best thing for the troops at that point was to see someone reacting in a human way.[28]

Chaplain Clapper, without knowing it, had exercised significant grief leadership by exposing his own human response, which in turn told the unit that it was OK to "lose it" at times. The following Sunday a worship service was held on the grass behind the dining hall on the base. The commander of the unit demonstrated his own humanity by briefly recounting how he had "pulled the plug" on his emotions and let all the tears out. He then went on to encourage the other members of the unit to do the same.

The way we bring healing to ourselves after a traumatic time in our lives is to find others who are struggling with the same tragedies or pains. Our venting and exposing how we have been hurt by the crisis bring healing to ourselves and others. I once heard that we are not to waste our sorrows. Wherever the phrase originated, the insight is substantially true. Our sorrows should not be kept to ourselves. We can nurse our hurts for all they are worth but never adequately recover from them until we begin to take the sword of healing to others. When the ugly realities of life and death rob us of our joy and lust for life, we must turn outward, find others who share similar pain, and jointly seek to beautify the world.

How many organizations exist today because one traumatized victim decided not to wallow in pain and despair but to make a difference in someone else's life? Alcoholics Anonymous, Mothers Against Drunk Drivers, victim-assistance groups, rape-counseling organizations all have their genesis in the traumatized who refused to bury their experience. They realized that if they had been hurt, abused, or misunderstood by their experiences, then there were others who shared the same pain. Together they could heal.

A story is told about a man who got lost in the woods. After circling for days on end without success, he sat down and wept. Soon he heard a rustling in the trees. Another man emerged out of the dense thicket. The first man asked, "Can you help me out of the woods?" The newfound friend replied, "No, I can't, but I'll walk along with you." This is the kind of assistance the victim has to offer. He may not be out of the woods in his own life, but he offers to walk with another victim through a shared journey. In the journey and the walking together healing takes place.

It's always so amazing to me how modern research confirms ancient wisdom. In the New Testament, Saul of Tarsus recorded for his readers a similar kind of grief leadership . . . a grief leadership that comes from God, which we in turn receive and then share with others. The apostle wrote:

> Blessed be the God and Father of our Lord Jesus Christ, the Father of mercies and God of all comfort, who comforts us in all our tribulation, that we may be able to comfort those who are in any trouble, with the comfort with which we ourselves are comforted by God (2 Cor. 1:3–4).

Here the principle is again affirmed: we help ourselves by helping others. Our own healing is linked to sharing what has worked for us with others in similar need.

Can you imagine the trauma of receiving a call from the police and being told that your son has just shot someone? You knew he was not well, but you also thought you were doing right by giving him the best mental-health care money could buy. But the phone call still comes as a surprise: "It's my son who has shot someone. Why?" But then the real blow hits. The person he shot was the president of the United States! Jack Hinckley could have done many things: disowned his son, blamed his psychiatrist, felt personally responsible for being a too-busy executive and not close enough to his son's problems. All the above were probably true at some point in his initial response. But Jack Hinckley decided to take the sword to others. He resigned from his company and began the American Mental Health Fund with limited funds to try to help other families struggling to understand the mental problems of their loved ones. This is what it means to find healing in helping.

Throughout this chapter I have tried to point out what researchers and those who work in the field of trauma have learned from the walking wounded. They are the survivors. They have survived because they have felt the human touch when they needed it. They began to regain control of their out-of-control world. A sense of meaning and purpose for their pain was found, and they killed the dragon of guilt. Finally, they started to reach out to others and found healing in helping other fellow sufferers. Regardless of the trauma, however, everyone asks the one fundamental question at one time or another: Why, God? Whether or not we like it, whether or not we are religious, everyone eventually wrestles with God over the traumas in his life. Why do we ask why? The why question brings us face-to-face with some tough theological issues that are rarely addressed by the mental-health professionals, even though they deal with the symptoms of these issues daily. Where does God fit into all this?

To you whose names are on this wall
I am sorry I couldn't be God
If I were God, if there were a God,
there would be no need for such a wall.
Dusty
A Vietnam Nurse at the
Memorial[1]

The reality of grief is the absence of God.
William Sloane Coffin[2]

Think not thou canst sigh a sigh
And thy maker is not by;
Think not thou canst weep a tear
And thy maker is not near.
William Blake
"On Another's Sorrow"[3]

C H A P T E R   5

What Our Scream Says About God

A tragedy such as the Delta 191 crash at Dallas-Fort Worth makes one very aware of the human response to trauma. Dealing with people of all religious and nonreligious faiths was quite a challenge for a protestant chaplain. Even though, as military chaplains, we are trained to work exclusively within our own faith groups (Catholic, protestant, Greek Orthodox, and Jewish), in mass-casualty situations there is often not the time or personnel to do the proper thing. Consequently, I often found myself counseling, grieving, or being with someone of a radically different religious background. In addition, on every flight of a modern jetliner there exists in that small cocoon in the sky a slice of the world's diversity. On flight 191 there were Jews, Catholics, Hindus, Buddhists, atheists, agnostics, born-again Christians, New Agers, the nonreligious, and the undecided. What intrigued me throughout the week of dealing with these fellow grievers was that they all asked the same theological question: "Why did God allow this to happen?" It's the question of meaning again but this time in a much deeper and more foundational way. Here the assumption was a recognition that God somehow still governs our world and is capable of preventing such tragedies as air crashes. Many psychologists would just call these questions emotional reactions, but are they? I certainly agree that they are initial emotional reactions, but I also believe they are more than that. I expect such questions from the religious and seminary students, but from across the spectrum of diversity found on any airplane in the sky this surprised me. The question gets at whether there are ultimate meanings.

Trauma also raises several other theological issues that traumatic-stress studies are now beginning to recognize. Frankl was probably one of the first in the psychiatric field to acknowledge this. He questioned:

> And what about man? Are you sure that the human world is a terminal point in the evolution of the cosmos? Is it not conceivable that there is still another dimension, a world beyond man's world; a world in which the question of an ultimate meaning of human suffering would find an answer?[4]

At some point the therapist, friend, relative, or pastor must realize that when trauma shatters the worldview, it brings the issue of God and the issue of ultimate meaning into the picture. Our scream is a scream against God. To miss this dimension is to miss the primal reaction of humankind. The issues of trauma are theological in nature. The first question raises the meaning of meaning.

What Is the Meaning of Meaning?

In chapter 4 it was observed that survival is related to finding some meaning in the pain or trauma. This is commonly recognized among the professionals working in the field. What is interesting to me, though, is how these same professionals who so openly value the role of a functional, personal meaning in order to cope with immediate struggles sometimes devalue any significance to larger ultimate meanings. It is as if "any ol' meaning will do," as long as it gets one through the immediate stages of recovery. However, with more reflection on the nature of meaning we are pressed back into philosophical and anthropological studies. Now I am no philosopher, but I do think we can learn something about the nature of human beings by the questions they ask, even to themselves. Why do humans wrestle with meaning and are in despair when meaning is absent? I don't know for sure, but I do believe we reflect our natures. If God is a meaningful Creator, and somehow He has brought into being this amazing creature called humankind, then there must be some connection between the way God is and the way humankind functions. If God is the ultimate meaning in the universe, and He has made humans in His image (which the Bible says), then people must have some innate sense that they are made for more than mere functionality. We look for meaningful relationships because we are meaningful creatures. Meaning is attached to our personhood, who we are and why we exist. Without a sense of meaning we perish. As Frankl has said, "He who has a why to live can bear with almost any how."[5]

Some might ask, "Why is it important to have an ultimate meaning?" It would seem to me that most of our temporary or functional meanings that we find in our pains will only fail us, given enough time. The POW may gain daily strength in the fact that he has a family waiting for him. The value and meaning of his family keep him alive for years. But when he returns, he finds that his wife has divorced him, his kids don't know him, and his sustaining temporary meaning has been abolished. The meaning he found for staying alive is then gone, and he enters an entirely new trauma—all because he had not linked personal meaning to some ultimate meaning.

The struggle to find ultimate meaning that includes God often takes extreme forms. Soon after the initial wave of families had poured into the Hilton Hotel, a young stewardess approached me. She had come to give assistance. When she saw the cross on my uniform, she asked, "Are you a Christian?" I replied, "Yes." Then she blurted out, "I know why God allowed this plane to crash." I responded, "You do?" "Yes," she explained, "you see, I just found out that a businessman was on that plane traveling with another woman under his wife's name." Since the plane was bound for Las Vegas, the weekend getaway appeared to her as a typical lover's affair. The stewardess left as quickly as she approached, but after she left, I found myself asking, "Is this the kind of God we have, one who would take 137 lives in order to zap one man sneaking away for a weekend with another woman?" The stewardess was grappling with ultimate meanings all right, but perhaps she was trying to find more meaning in the tragedy than was actually there.

But again, her struggle illustrates our need for ultimate meaning.

A few days later, a Dallas newspaper carried on the front page a headline saying, "Chaplain says, 'God had nothing to do with it.'" The article focused on one hospital chaplain's struggle to try to absolve God from blame for the crash. I also appreciated his struggle for meaning. I too had wrestled in my own understanding over such loss of life. However, it seemed to me that my fellow chaplain's "explanation" to the press only presented more problems than it solved. In his struggle for meaning he had gotten rid of all meaning. By the long-standing notions of who God is, if God is not in some mysterious way involved in everything, then He is not involved in anything. My chaplain friend had too little meaning for any griever to find comfort in.

So where does this leave us? Somewhere between too much meaning and not enough. My bias on this subject stands within the parameters of the historic Judeo-Christian position, which affirms that God in His infinite wisdom continues to sustain and guide the world, and therefore everything that happens has intrinsic meaning and purpose. It is God who brings about our well-being through many various means and who brings about calamity (Isa. 45:7). It is God who gives health and prosperity (Deut. 28:11), and it is God who allows the dumb, deaf, and blind to be born (Ex. 4:11). Even Job, in the midst of his trauma, recalled this perspective by saying to his wife, "Shall we indeed accept good from God, and shall we not accept adversity?" (Job 2:10). However, to hold this position does not mean that every person can specifically know why a particular trauma occurred. I think it is very unwise even to speculate about such things. I may believe in a God who has a meaning and purpose for all that happens, but to believe that I know what that specific purpose is to border on an encroachment of the divine. I am not God. I will never know what purposes He may have when babies die, or women are raped, or air crashes take innocent lives. But because I can't fully understand these purposes does not mean that the better position is to see no purpose at all. As Phillip Yancey has said so well, "The alternative to disappointment with God seems to be disappointment without God."[6]

Since the Enlightenment it has been increasingly difficult for Western people to accept the reality that all our hopes and dreams will not be realized in this life. Conversely, with industrialization and new technological developments, many thought that all pain and suffering would be eliminated. What many are now realizing is that we live in a fragile world, we are finite beings, and many things happen that await explanation only in the next life. Trauma, in some benevolent way, reminds us of who we are. We are human and not God, but God is our only connection to ultimate meaning. God may not reveal to us in any sufficient way why our traumas have happened, but to try to work through the depth of despair without God is even more difficult. God may not be an all-sufficient answer for us, for it is better than no answer at all!

Even death seems like such an intrusion. It is! Within our very beings there is something that screams, crying out that we are made for more than what is here. When death, disease, and calamities hit us, why is it that we just can't somewhat passively accept these as realities of life? No, we fight them because they are intrusions. Something within us knows that this is not right; it's not the way the world was made or necessarily the way it will remain forever. The meaning of meaning places us face-to-face with ourselves and God. In our warfare we affirm the very thing we would like to deny. We rage against Him, deny Him, all the time affirming His existence in our struggle with Him.

But other issues spring forth from this foundational one. The most prominent one is, of course, the problem of evil.

If God Is Good, Why Is There Evil?

When psychotherapy was first born, it seems that almost all psychic pain found its explanation in the heart of one's mother. Whatever a person's ills, the mother was to blame. It was not an era when personal responsibility for problems or difficulties was taken. Blame was placed elsewhere.[7] But in the early seventies Karl Menninger set a new course in psychotherapy with the publication of his book *Whatever Became of Sin?* Before this, sin had not been in the psychological textbooks. Evil existed only in one's mind or in the way one was raised but certainly not in the heart of every person. With this radical approach Menninger took the first step away from the Enlightenment era, which in popular fashion said, "Take no personal responsibility for your failures." In the aftermath of Menninger's reversal the mental-health field largely followed suit and for the past several decades has given serious attention to taking responsibility for one's own life and problems. It wasn't called bearing responsibility for one's own sins, but it called for taking more responsibility for one's problems and healing.

Then in 1983 M. Scott Peck, a well-published psychiatrist (*The Road Less Traveled*), wrote *People of the Lie: the Hope for Healing Human Evil.* In the mental-health community it was an atomic bomb. A psychiatrist talking about evil and evil people! The categories are not found in the DSM III listing of psychiatric disorders. Peck admits that the book is not a nice book because it is about our dark side and about the very darkest members of our human community.[8] I still remember finishing reading the book, turning to my wife, and saying, "The next step is for the concept of hell to be brought back into the public square of knowledge." Over a year ago my words seemed prophetic. In the middle of an apparent love story gone bad, a man, after killing someone and then dying himself, is dragged off by demon spirits to the sounds of screaming and gnashing of teeth. The movie, *Ghost,* in this particular scene could have been something out of the biblical Apocalypse. Evil is back in vogue, but how does this fit with the concept of a good God? Sooner or later, every victim tries to reframe the evil with how God can fit into the picture of life-threatening traumas.

At this point I feel that the mental-health community has gone as far as it can go without acknowledging some deeper and more insidious power at work in human suffering. Evil confronts us with choices, and for the most part we don't like the available options. In the past, evil was denied altogether as a mental-health aberration. Today some who admit its real existence would rather live as though it doesn't exist or just not think about it. This is what the character Casey, a renegade preacher, does in Steinbeck's *Grapes of Wrath.* He says, "There ain't no sin and there ain't no virtue. . . . There's just stuff people do."[9] Well, sometimes the things people do, when done to us, are not adequately explained in this view. It feels like evil; it is evil. Just to say that it is what people do diminishes the nature and intensity of the felt horror. Try telling a woman who has been raped that it's just what men do. Tell the man who has lost his whole family in the Holocaust that this is just what people do. It doesn't work. It makes a mockery of pain, horror, and human agony. It lessens the reality of what happened. Let's call it what it is—evil. But, then, how could God allow it?

At this point some may ask, "But can you put these kinds of moral evils (human injustice) in the same category with such things as earthquakes, floods, or even plane crashes, where there is no apparent human error?" Surely, natural evils are of a different category than the human-injustice ones. Again, try explaining to someone whose house has just burned down that it was only a natural evil. When a child dies in a flood, it really doesn't make any difference to the parent whether it was a moral evil or a natural evil. These are the things that concern only ivory-tower theologians. John Stuart Mill stated it rather bluntly but realistically:

> Nature impales men, breaks them as if on the wheel, casts them to be devoured by wild beasts, burns them to death, crushes them with stones, starves them with hunger, freezes them with cold, poisons them by the quick or slow venom of her exhalations and has hundreds of other hideous deaths in reserve.[10]

Denial of evil may work until the evil strikes close to home. When it does, we become instant believers in the problem of evil. But does this mean that God has become impotent, or took a vacation, or momentarily took his eyes off the world? We all want a solution to this dilemma. I will not solve it for you. Theologians and philosophers through the ages have wrestled with the problem without any final answer. No, I won't solve it. But neither will the psychologists, therapists, New Agers, or anyone else, for that matter.

Unless you live with your head in the sand, I believe we must admit that evil exists and is real. Many of the traumatic events we face in life are the very confrontation with evil. This seems to be the only adequate explanation for the depth of horror aroused by such things as multiple losses of life, torture, mutilation, and so on. At the same time, as meaningful creatures we look for some meaning even in the worst tragedies in order to find some reason to keep on living. This search for meaning puts us on the track of a Godward search. Where is the God who allows this to happen? Perhaps this God is very much present in our pain and in mysterious ways has much deeper purposes in it than we can ever realize. The recognition of ultimate meaning and purpose is always a declaration of faith. Tragedy is not good, and it seems to call into question either the goodness of God or the omnipotence of God. To affirm the goodness of God in the midst of the worst evil is to affirm something that many view as irrational or absurd. From a purely Aristotelian, logical point of view, it may be. But logic does not really have the ability to factor in the mysterious purposes of God. As difficult as it may be to make this kind of affirmation against all sensibilities, my concern is that attempts to find meaning without any ultimate purposes will ultimately fail. In my opinion, they are doomed to fail and will never bring about adequate healing. In order to reframe the worst traumatic events, there exists in the heart of humankind the need to find a greater, deeper purpose. Even knowing that there is a larger purpose for what happened, though the specific purpose is not known, has given many throughout the ages the strength to go on.

In an interview with Rose Kennedy, when asked how she has been able to survive the multiple traumas of her life, she replied almost without thinking, "My faith . . . my faith in a God who is good and who will not allow anything to happen to me that I can't get through." Is this just the wishful thinking of an old, religious woman that has given her the pragmatic ability to cope with the loss of three sons, one husband, and one son-in-law and to work through the traumas of having a mentally retarded daughter and of seeing a grandson's leg amputated? I say no. There is real meaning here. Someone is really there who gives meaning and brings healing even in the midst of evil.

But what about those who have done evil things to themselves or others? It seems that their battle is more with themselves than with God.

Implications of Moral Guilt

There's an old story about a grown man who had a problem with bed-wetting. He always felt embarrassed and guilty about it. He finally confided in a friend, who told him that he should talk to a therapist. After many months of therapy his friend asked him about his problem. The man said, "Everything is fine." His friend rejoiced, saying, "Then you're healed." "No," the man said, "I just don't feel guilty about it anymore!" In some counseling approaches this has often been the case. The goal has been to rid the person of guilt because guilt was usually deemed an unhealthy mental condition arising from too strict an unbringing or too many societal expectations. In other words, guilt was purely a psychological mechanism not founded in deviation from or a breach of moral principles. But when it comes to dealing with some issues in traumatic stress, it seems true that moral guilt has become a serious issue. It raises a profoundly theological concern about the nature of right and wrong.

In the early stages after Vietnam, the mental-health approach was to tell veterans who felt guilty that they were merely following orders or that they were serving their country. Therefore, they should not feel guilty. But it was observed that many were drinking themselves to death, destroying their marriages, and sabotaging their careers. Why? Underneath the veterans' exterior was a deep-seated conflict of conscience. Many had done things they were deeply ashamed of. They couldn't understand how they could have done such things as killing their own officers or killing women and children. One F-105 pilot asked me during the war what I thought about dropping napalm on villages. He was always flying so fast that he never saw what the napalm did, but he knew what it could do and whom he was dropping it on. His conscience was beginning to bother him. Was this the result of having been raised in too strict a family or of society's morality about killing innocents? No, the research suggests something much deeper here. Hendin and Haas, while discussing why some veterans survived Vietnam without as many problems, commented on their apparent absence of guilt:

> Consistent with the fact that the veterans who did not develop posttraumatic stress had maintained a high degree of emotional and intellectual control during their combat and were not

turned on by violence, their combat histories were characterized by an absence of actions over which they felt or needed to
deny guilt. Specifically, none in the group had engaged in non-
military killings of civilians, prisoners, or other Americans; in
sexual abuse; or in mutilation of enemy dead. Since, as we
discussed earlier, such actions and subsequent guilt were so
frequent among veterans with posttraumatic stress disorders,
their absence among the men we are discussing here is
significant.

We have also seen that guilt is frequently found among combat
soldiers whose killing was strictly within an official military
context. Among those with posttraumatic stress we have
found this guilt to be related to experiencing killing as a more
than usual source of excitement or expression of rage. In
contrast, the veterans in the non-posttraumatic stress group
tended to kill enemy soldiers with a sense of reluctance, experiencing relatively little guilt afterward.[11]

This research records the psychological impact of maintaining a sense of morality during warfare. It also speaks
perhaps of a deeper law inherent in our personhood. Some
things are inherently wrong (like killing innocents or maiming
human beings), and consequently, when we do them, a deep-
seated violation of our consciences takes place. The guilt we
feel is because we are guilty of horrible crimes against our
fellowman. To feel this guilt is to be human; not to feel it is
inhuman. Figley's research points out how destructive this
sense of guilt is when left as it is:

Two kinds of psychiatric syndromes among veterans have
been described. One is a "numbed guilt" reaction, which con-
sists of an unarticulated guilt generated by "atrocity" experiences, and manifested in psychic numbing, a need to victimize
others, touchiness, suspiciousness, and withdrawal.[12]

117

The guilt these vets feel is, in my own explanation, true moral guilt. It can't be explained away, soothed away, or even psychoanalyzed away. If its existence is woven into the fabric of our human personalities, then it is very much a theological as well as a psychological problem. If the problem has theological roots, then its solution must also have a theological orientation as well.

I don't in any way want to oversimplify the problem of guilt. Many punish themselves for many reasons other than true moral guilt. I do accept the reality of scapegoating, or feeling guilty because of having an unaffirming parent or serving as an enabling personality to an alcohol or drug addict, which makes the person feel a sense of guilt. But in the clear practice of a moral wrong against another human being, I believe we are dealing with things that the psychological approach long has ignored.

What, then, is the cure for true moral guilt? The answer common among therapists today is self-forgiveness. Anyone who has committed what she considers moral wrongs needs self-forgiveness. However, I question whether telling someone that she needs to forgive herself has any particular power to it. Is the nature of forgiveness something that comes from inside a human being or from without? I can have an argument with my wife and say some things I don't mean that really hurt her. Once I realize what I have done, I feel badly about it because I wronged her. Now at this point I could just say to myself, *I forgive myself for what I did.* I have met veterans who are still walking around saying this to themselves, but inside they are punishing themselves for their own wrong. They obviously have not appropriated a sense of forgiveness merely by saying to themselves, *I forgive me.* What is needed? For me to experience forgiveness, it must come from without. I must go back to my wife, admit my wrong, and ask *her* to forgive me. Once she says, "I forgive you," then I can begin to feel forgiven. I don't believe self-forgiveness is possible until we have been forgiven by someone outside ourselves.

At this point it would be great if there were some way veterans could be told by our society or by the Republic of Vietnam that they are forgiven. But this is probably not possible. For soldiers who maimed bodies or fragged their own officers, I think it would be very therapeutic to go to the families of such people and ask for forgiveness. But in most cases this is both unreasonable and impossible. However, our crimes against humanity are also crimes against God's moral standards. That's why we feel the way we feel. Therefore, the point to begin is with God. Chaim Shatan, founder of the Vietnam Veterans Working Group, wrote:

> Veterans will often ask, "How do we turn off the guilt? Can we atone? Why didn't we get killed, rather than carry out illegal orders?" Their own answers follow quickly: They speak of "paying their dues" for surviving unscathed when others did not survive. They invite self-punishment by picking self-defeating fights, inviting rejection from near ones, even getting involved in a remarkably high number of single-car, single-occupant accidents.[13]

Did you notice the language? "Atone, punish." This is the language of the veteran and all those who are wrestling with their moral wrongs. These terms have their origins in the theological community. The veteran, in the absence of society's punishing him for the wrongs he has committed, punishes himself. In some strange way this is the response of the human psyche about its moral wrongs. Deep within us we know that our remedies for guilt are punishment and some form of atonement. In the absence of atonement from without, we create our own. We make our own hell, serve our own time, create our own punishment. Some veteran centers have become proactive on this concept. Instead of telling the veteran to forgive himself, they are now saying, "For what you did in 'nam, how much punishment would be sufficient?" Forty lashes with a whip, or two years in jail, or five years of community service?" This is not in jest. Some therapists actively work with veterans to get them to set goals through which they can achieve a sense of having finished their "penance" for moral wrongs. Having finished their time of punishment, they can then forgive themselves. As beneficial as this can be, I still believe the main point has been missed. Our crimes are not only against our fellowman but also against God. But what has God done about our crimes? Ramsey has observed that down to the year A.D. 1000 every private soldier had to do forty days of penance for fighting in any war, no matter how just. Perhaps the ancient warriors knew more about warfare and the human condition afterward than we do today.[14]

It is interesting to me, as one trained in both the theological and psychological sciences, how often the two fields meet today. The word *atone,* now commonly used in VA treatment programs, first appears in the Jewish Bible. The Jewish community celebrates as its most holy of days Yom Kippur, the Day of Atonement. What was this day? This was not a day when the community gathered together to find "self-forgiveness," but it was *the* day when the community came together to experience the forgiveness that could come only from God. On that day animals were slaughtered as an atonement for the impurities, trans-gressions, and sins of the people of Israel (see Lev. 16—17). Aaron, the high priest, also would confess over the head of a live goat all the iniquities of the community and then have the animal released into the wilderness as a scapegoat for the people (see Lev. 16:21). For the people it was a time of sabbath rest and humbling their souls before God (see Lev. 16:29). The result was: "On that day the priest shall make atonement for you, to cleanse you, that you may be clean from all your sins before the LORD" (Lev. 16:30). Today in the absence of a place to practice this rite properly, the Jewish community spends the day in prayer, meditation, and fasting to start the new year with a clear conscience. But it is still a time of both asking forgiveness of one another and believing that God forgives on the basis of their charitable works toward one another.[15] The concept here is that forgiveness comes from without by the means of an animal's substituting and bearing the penalty for the crimes committed throughout the year by the person. In theology it is called substitutionary atonement. We don't atone for our own sins; something else atones *for* us. Forgiveness must come from without before it can come from within. Some theologians see this concept of an atoning animal sacrifice as nothing more than a primitive attempt to appease an offended deity. However, it is my opinion that as one reads the passages about this holy day, the focus is more on what the sacrifice is to do for the people than on God. If God is appeased by the sacrifice, that is beside the point. The major concern is the benefit of people and their cleansing.

A second important concept that emerges from the Jewish Scriptures is that a person can also atone for another's wrongs. The prophet Isaiah envisions a suffering Servant who takes upon Himself an atonement for others. This one is a Man of pains, knowing fully the experience of grief. The prophet wrote:

Surely He has borne our griefs
And carried our sorrows;
Yet we esteemed Him stricken,
Smitten by God, and afflicted.
But He was wounded for our transgressions,
He was bruised for our iniquities;
The chastisement for our peace was upon Him,
And by His stripes we are healed. . . .
And the LORD has laid on Him the iniquity of us all. . . .
Yet it pleased the LORD to bruise Him;
He has put Him to grief.
When You make His soul an offering for sin (Isa. 53:4–6, 10).

Notice the words: *offering, stripes, smitten, wounded, bruised, grief.* These are the punishments many victims of traumatic events put themselves through because they cannot rid themselves of their own guilt. In this passage the prophet envisioned a man's bearing the punishment for those deserving such. The point is that because this Servant has borne the punishment, the transgressor does not have to.

I must admit that this interpretation has not been universally received by those in the Jewish community. Because Christians have claimed this passage as speaking of Jesus Christ, my Jewish friends reject the concept of substitutionary atonement for them. But it is their passage, and my feeling is that the passage cannot be reconciled with the standard Jewish interpretation that it speaks of Israel and not their Messiah. It is to Israel that this individual is revealed (see Isa. 53:1). In the Christian community the passage is believed to find its fulfillment in the person of the One who claimed to be the Jewish Messiah, Jesus. (*Jesus Christ* means "Jesus the Messiah" or "Anointed One.") The Christian Scriptures clearly teach that "in Him [Jesus] we have redemption [release from our wrongs] through His blood, the forgiveness of sins" (Eph. 1:7).

I remember once talking to a former Catholic priest who told me that he could no longer believe in a God who demanded sacrifices. I asked him, "How, then, can you say that anyone is forgiven if there is no longer any atonement?" He just looked at me. Finally, he said, "I guess I can't." From the psychological community we are finding that self-punishment is not working. How many community projects does one have to do to find his own forgiveness? How many marriages must a veteran break apart before he has had enough self-punishment? There's an interesting irony here. Just at the time many in the psychological fields are very open to theological forgiveness, some in the theological communities no longer believe in a God who forgives on the basis of atonement. Forgiveness begins with the recognition that God has provided atonement for all humankind.[16] The punishment due us has been placed on another. Therefore, I do not have to punish myself or put myself on a never-ending search for an appropriate penance.

Another axiom of modern psychotherapy is that of giving hope. Whether or not it is realized, here again the concept of hope places us in theological territory.

Hope as a Theological Issue

I've taken a lot of counseling courses, and I've read much on the subject of counseling. I'm always amazed when

I find what seems like uniform agreement in a field that is not an exact science. Almost per book or course every counselor would agree, "Never let the client leave without a sense of hope." Whether it is for fear of being sued if one commits suicide, I don't know. But the practice is fairly axiomatic for the field. I have often felt the bind myself in trying to be hopeful. I have had cases that caused me to say to myself, *This person or situation is hopeless!* I would catch myself, knowing that I should never say that, and then try to figure out how in the world I could find hope for this person. As I have talked to other counselors, they readily agree to similar binds. So why must we be purveyors of hope? I would suggest that hope is a theological concept that has been stolen by the mental-health establishment and then secularized. It has also been largely stolen and popularized by almost all motivational speakers who specialize in convincing their audiences that the impossible dreams are possible and that within every human being is another Horatio Alger waiting to be born. Just as the search for meaning is so critical to surviving traumas, so is having a sense of hope. In fact, our sense of hope grows from having a meaning, so they are deeply related to each other. So what is the hope for the traumatized?

The traumatized see no hope, yet they need hope in order to survive. The secular hope is that of personal development. In the reframing process of recovery what is usually suggested is that somehow the individual will see how the trauma has given a new perspective or brought about an element of personal growth. This is so much a part of the therapeutic assumptive world today that I find it is rarely critiqued. It is assumed by everyone that if we can find some area in which we have grown, then whatever has happened to us is justified. This is our hope, that we will be better people because we have gone through so much. Now I believe it is true that people grow through their difficulties. I accept the reality that we *may* be better people for going through extreme difficulty, but I don't believe this should be the all-controlling hope. This kind of goal merely gets down to reestablishing a sense of well-being, which is a hope based purely at the individual, temporal level. Christopher Lasch has seriously critiqued this type of thinking. In talking about this awareness movement, he wrote:

> The contemporary climate is therapeutic, not religious. People today hunger not for personal salvation, let alone for the restoration of an earlier golden age, but for the feeling, the momentary illusion, of personal well-being, health and psychic security.... The ideology of personal growth, superficially optimistic, ultimately radiates a profound despair and resignation. It is the faith of those without faith.[17]

Did you see what he calls this secularized, therapeutic faith? "Superficially optimistic." This is the secular hope. It looks for good feelings, contentment, and psychic peace. But these are the superficial, "come-on" kinds of hope offered in most counseling offices. For those who have been severely traumatized I believe these are trivial hopes to build and reconstruct lives upon. They are hopes that will disappoint with time.

Another form of secular hope is that of reincarnation. In the pattern of typical Eastern mysticism the ground argument lies in recognizing that there is no hope in this world. This world is mere preparation for the next. Respond well to difficulty here, and maybe you will find advancement in the next life as some higher, more well-developed being. This is merely the personal-growth hope given a new twist. We can't be all we can be here, so our hope is in being reincarnated as something better! It may be an improvement over the first false hope in the sense that it at least recognizes that all our earthly hopes will disappoint. However, I have many other problems with the concept of reincarnation on both theological grounds and as a hope-providing technique for the traumatized. New Age reincarnation seems to attract a following among those who delight in having been someone famous in the past, but the future-hope element is not that well articulated. The reality of karma is that one could equally be reincarnated as an ant, a mouse, or an endangered species. Personally, that's a more fearful hope to me than believing in hell!

If these secular hopes are not sufficient as a basis for healing the traumatized, where can a more sufficient hope be based? Again, I return to the long-standing themes of Judeo-Christianity. Hope has been and always will be a theologically rooted concept. When God created the world, it was very good (see Gen. 1:31). Whether this was the best of all possible worlds is not clear and, of course, is impossible to prove.[18] The tradition also affirms that humankind lost this first relation and fell into a condition in which pain, discomfort, injustice, and inhumanity became commonplace throughout history. Throughout this history God has constantly intervened through His prophets to give humankind a hope from above. The vision of the future from the prophet Isaiah to the Apocalypse of John is one of a latter-day hope in which God will restore the earth to a condition of peace, harmony, prosperity, and justice. It will be a time when the voice of weeping will no longer be heard, and the wolf and the lamb will feed together (see Isa. 65:19, 25). It will be a time of healing for everyone, when every tear will be wiped away, and mourning and death will no longer exist (see Rev. 21:3–4; 22:2).

Is this a pie-in-the-sky hope? No, it is not. It is the only real hope we as humankind have. It is the source of all hope. All earthly hopes ultimately disappoint, whether they be jobs, careers, bank accounts, marriages, children, churches, or civic contributions. They will all fade in time. The only hope that does not disappoint is one that is not based or found in time and space as we know it. Again, it is apprehended and envisioned only through the eyes of faith. Paul of Tarsus wrote to some of these believers who were living in the city of cities, the capital of the world, Rome. In short, he told them that their traumas *do* produce a certain steadfastness and proved character. Trials do make us stronger as persons. But he concluded by saying that their traumas ultimately bring forth an important element of hope, and this is a hope that does not disappoint. What is this hope? That our God invades us from without and manifests His love for us in our hearts (see Rom. 5:5). Because He has established this relationship with us, He will not leave us as orphans but will receive us unto Himself either through death or at the end of time (see John 14:1–3).

Phil Garcia, a Vietnam veteran, referred to this hope when he said:

I got tired of being my own god. I had a complete mental breakdown when I left the post office. I couldn't support my family; I had to fight with the Veterans Administration to get my disability pension reinstated. The experience turned me back to my old Judeo-Christian beliefs. I stopped seeing man as being able to save himself.[19]

There exists today an amazing paradox. On one end of the self-help spectrum are all of the motivational tapes, books, and seminars that convince you that you can do anything. This is the human-potential movement at its finest. It finds its most enthusiastic adherents in the business world, especially those in high-commission sales. This material has some helpful material and has kept many adherents functioning with positive mind-sets. At the other end of the self-help counter is another type of literature and tapes. These are the addiction, dysfunctional-family, codependency, abuse, and eating- and sexual-disorder books. This material has as its foundational premise for recovery "You can't do it." Some, like AA, go even further and say that hope is not within the human potentiality but outside in some higher power. Both types of these books sell, and sell well. However, it seems that very few question the fact that the premises of the two movements diametrically oppose each other. The human-potential people say, "Your hope is within you. You can do it." The step programs for overcoming addictions and disorders say, "You can't do it. You need outside help." Now someone is either wrong here or at least not interacting with the other side of the movement.

Frankly, I believe that the hope we place in our own human potential is faulty, if not dangerous. It is a never-ending street. How does one know if she has ever fully developed her potential? At least a dead-end street forces one to stop and think about alternatives. The self-help, human-potential movement just keeps making more promises that we can be more than we are right now. It breeds dissatisfaction by making unrealistic promises. In my opinion, it is secular snake oil! The concept sets up people for being suckered into anything that a motivational speaker believes strongly enough will help develop the person further . . . usually for a price! The result is that we usually end up condemning ourselves for not achieving the impossible demands of someone else's definition of what it means to be fully developed. Besides, behind every potential Horatio Alger is also a potential Adolf Hitler. Does this sound extreme? I don't think so.

True hope is an absurd hope. It is a hope that confronts us and encourages us even when the world is totally absurd. It is a hope that takes evil seriously and doesn't gloss over it with high-sounding potentialities from well-healed motivational speakers. It is a hope that emerges from the absurd precisely because it is not rooted in the earthly dreams of human potentiality. It is a more realistic hope because it is *not* based in the here and now. It is what Frankl has called a "tragic optimism" simply because it is optimism in the face of tragedy.[20] It is optimism because it transports the individual out of the present and allows him to see beyond the tragedy to a hope on the other side. It is the hope that Dietrich Bonhoeffer, a German pastor, had as the Nazis placed a noose around his neck with the liberating Russian armies in sight.[21] It is the hope that Joni Eareckson has had in overcoming her paraplegic state and learning to paint and write with a pencil in her mouth. It is the hope that gave Aleksandr Solzhenitsyn the motive for detailing the daily experiences in the Russian Gulags. It is the hope that has kept alive the Eastern-bloc churches for over half a century.

Yes, this hope is not based on earthly dreams of utopia, or on personal dreams of well-being, or on having a hot tub in every bedroom. It is a hope for the traumatized that comes from the traumatized. It is a hope that comes from the future and invades the present. It is a hope that throughout history has been the hope of the nations in the Prince of Peace who is also the Prince of Pain. This is the One who said He would return to this earth, gather His people, and judge the earth for all its vindictiveness and evil. This is not a popular concept today. However, no matter how romantic our notion of the "wrongness" of judgment, it must be admitted that purely human judgment for evil is severely lacking. Every day in our justice system the wrong person is acquitted, and another innocent is punished. The system itself raises a fundamental theo-logical question about the nature of hope. A genuine hope necessitates the righting of wrongs and the sufficient punishment of evildoers. I personally do not want to play God in this matter and make the determination. However, I feel that there exists a theological necessity for some ultimate dealing with all the injustices of the world. In this regard, I trust neither those who are conservative, who would like to usurp this role, nor those who are liberal, who would like to do away with the whole concept of judicial punishment. Wrong, evil, and injustice demand punishment and ultimate confrontation by a truly fair and impartial judge.

Personally, my hope for this justice lies not in this world but in divine reckoning. I don't believe a Hitler should get away with his murderous crimes by merely putting a gun to his head and thus avoiding all justice. This to me is the worst kind of injustice, one which the romantic-enlightened liberal era has not adequately addressed. True hope must be rooted in the beyond, which deals with evil and injustice. As I write, the remains of Lt. Col. William Higgins, of the UN peacekeeping force, were finally dumped onto a street in Lebanon. In response his wife said, "There's got to be someone greater than you and me to judge a man who will kidnap, torture, and murder an unarmed United Nations peacekeeper.... I'm willing to wait for that judgment."[22] Mrs. Higgins's comment reflects what all the victimized feel. Earthly justice fails, so a part of the hope we need is for one that will accurately judge the injustice and bring true recompense. A hope like this can come only from above. This is what Jesus has promised. This is the message of the biblical prophets, and this is the desire of the traumatized. This hope is the promised hope, which becomes the basis of all the rest of our rehabilitative hopes.

The concept of this kind of hope leads us to another aspect of traumatic-stress studies that also raises some interesting theological issues.

Humanness as a Theological Concept

After spending the entire weekend at the Dallas-Fort Worth Hilton, I was naive enough to think that I could run into the city and teach my eight o'clock Monday-morning class at the seminary. Most of the survivors and families whom I had been working with through the weekend would sleep in and not get up until almost noon. So I drove into Dallas. I parked in my assigned faculty parking space and went up to my third-floor classroom. As I looked at my students and then down at my notes, I began to realize that something was wrong. I had taught the same class many times before, my notes were there, the students were there, but my mind wasn't connecting with my mouth. Finally, I decided to let my students know where I had been over the weekend. As I began to detail my time in the house of mourning with the families of 137 dead passengers, I began to sob. Finally, I realized I wasn't going to be able to teach my class. I told the students if they wanted an education, they would do better to come with me to the Dallas-Fort Worth Airport and serve as Red Cross volunteers. Some did.

Much later, I tried to understand what had happened in that classroom and why I had lost control of my emotions. I hadn't lost anyone on flight 191, so why was I crying? What I hadn't realized then is what I now know to be a very common "professional reaction" to trauma. I call it the Mai Tai malfunction. In Hawaii I'm told that a Mai Tai is a very syrupy, sweet, and powerful alcoholic drink. It goes down easily, and one never feels anything. After a while, though, it slips up on your blind side and totally knocks you out. This is what traumatic-stress situations often do to the professionals. All professional graduate schools teach students to departmentalize, not to feel or react, but to do the professional, medical, or psychological acts for others. This is a subtle form of denial of our own humanity. However, it is not nice to try to fool Mother Nature! Soon our humanity slips up on our blind side, and we are reminded very acutely and powerfully that we are what we are . . . human. As humans we were made by our Creator to feel, to grieve, to be angry, to be shocked by the horror we sometimes have to face. As professionals we departmentalize. We have our professional life, in which we don't feel or react, and then we have our private life, in which we laugh, cry, get depressed, and throw parties. For the most part, we can keep them divided until a major trauma hits or we are faced with a mass-casualty situation. In these cases it is sometimes the professional care-giver who gets overlooked and who sometimes has very serious problems. The problems are reminders that though a professional, she is still a member of the human race.

During the Delta crash I had several Parkland Hospital nurses tell me that they didn't know why they were having so many problems. They admitted that they had seen worse burn patients before, so it wasn't the severity of the medical problems. So why were they no longer able to keep the areas of their lives separate? My after-the-fact explanation centers on the nature of the event and the media. First, the nature of mass casualties is different from dealing with even the most severe individual cases. Most critical-care nurses have between eight and ten patients in their ward at a time. They go from bed to bed and do what needs to be done. Most are stabilized; therefore, it is relatively easy to manage even the worst patients. They may grieve from time to time over the death of a patient they got to know very well. (They grieve because the professional veil was pierced, and at that moment they became human.) But for the most part, when they go home, they no longer think about the patient. They can successfully keep their personal lives separate from their professional lives.

But in mass-casualty situations one can no longer neatly divide the areas of one's life. Reality breaks through to our humanity. The situation cannot be managed; there are more patients than nurses; key players are gone; phones are ringing; and the staff, though entirely competent in its usual routines, begins to break down. One hospital supervisor wrote me nine months after the crash and shared both her appreciation and concern for this area: "You were the only person who was able to identify burnout in yourself. Some of the worst offenders were the medical staff because they functioned as they would in a clinical setting."[23] Notice the words "worst offenders"... the professionals!

After the United Airlines crash in Sioux City an emergency-room supervisor wrote: "Many of us involved did not realize, nor were we prepared for, the extent of the emotional trauma we experienced that night. The psychological shock—our own, as well as that of the crash victims and their families—was something we had not rehearsed."[24] I have been on several military exercises where we rehearsed literally everything except what really happens in traumatic events. We used molage (makeup that gives the appearance of blood and open wounds) and fake victims, we had people yelling and screaming, we set aflame an old aircraft, and we practiced the whole routine of putting out the fire and responding to the victims. All the professional leadership was in place, functioning, directing, and responding appropriately. However, in the real situation many of them are gone, no longer capable of functioning because of burnout or other kinds of emotional collapse. Professionals are not supposed to scream, so their scream comes later. Usually it is quieter and less publicized and sometimes more complex because they are the professionals. The scream is God-given, a reminder that they are human, that it is human to scream at dead and mutilated bodies. These things are never rehearsed, and I'm not sure they really can be. Reality is always reality, which is hard to fake or prepare for.

To scream is to come face-to-face with our own humanity and personhood. To face ourselves is fundamentally a theological confrontation. As men and women made in the image of God, our emotions are reminders that we reflect something of God's feelings when we feel. Our rage at the inhumanness of a disaster is a reminder of how God may also rage at injustice, being a moral being. Not to rage at the severity of life is to function in a dehumanized way. It is to be less human and less than God made us. If this is difficult for the professionals, it is even more difficult for the untrained passersby who are often caught in the middle of certain traumatic events.

When a military disaster takes place, there are some tough jobs to be filled. Even though military personnel can be commanded to such roles, it is better to ask for volunteers. The volunteers a project officer gets are usually not trained in traumatic-stress studies. They are usually cooks, office personnel, and workers from a host of other career fields. Because certain tasks demand sheer numbers of people, mass volunteers are enlisted and sent to the disaster sites. Their job is to pick up all personal effects (luggage, records, equipment, weapons, and so on) and human remains. A mass of volunteers spreads out, covering the crash site (if a plane crash) and the surrounding area. The site is staked out and every grid given to a team. Once all the remains and personal effects are picked up, they go to Dover Air Force Base (Delaware) on the East Coast and Hickam Air Force Base (Hawaii) on the West. The bodies are then placed on portable tables on wheels, and the long process of body identification begins. Entire teams of medical examiners, dentists, pathologists, and FBI agents are called in to do the detailed analysis of fingerprints and teeth records.

Even for the professionals this is not an easy task. Chaplain Clapper recorded his morgue observations after the United Airlines crash in 1989:

Even the experienced personnel from the medical examiner's office, though, are confiding in me that it is extremely stressful for them. One tells me that when she is concentrating on one body she is okay, but she is overcome when she looks up and realizes the vast scale of it all (probably 6 or 8 autopsies going on at once, in addition to all of the other stages of the process—e.g. the people who take off the victims' clothes, the X-ray people, the fingerprinting people, the morticians, etc.). One person related to me one incident that was particularly stressful to her. She was doing the autopsy on one small child and she kept hearing people saying things like, "Isn't it terrible. . . ." She said that she was having a hard enough time with it herself without having to deal with the comments of others. Fortunately, she was able to stop what she was doing, order everybody away and get more protective screens brought in so she could finish in privacy.[25]

Medical examination is a distasteful process. Sometimes fingers have to be removed for proper fingerprint evaluation. Teeth must be carefully exposed or removed in order to get a proper match with dental reords. Is this necessary? Yes, on most civilian air flights the FBI estimates that at least 15 percent of the passengers are traveling under names other than their own. Even when billfolds and purses are still on the victims, it is not unusual for individuals to be carrying more than one person's driver's license or ID. Therefore, most identifications must be made by fingerprinting or dental records. In some cases in the Delta crash, identification was down to the level of having to identify passengers by means of a microscope.

I have tried to give you a picture of what takes place around a major traumatic event. Now imagine a volunteer or a passerby catching a glimpse of what is going on. Or imagine what it would be like to be one of the young volunteers at the Dover facility. Air Force Col. Robert Maloney has said that the "casualty" rate for volunteers is about 80 percent after the first few days.[26] The volunteers' job is to stay with the body through the various stages of examination. While the body is being examined, volunteers sit and watch what is going on.

The volunteers and professionals are the secondary victims of the trauma. They have not lost anyone personally, but through their work they begin to make human connections with the dead. I still vividly remember having to roll over my first corpse to look for identification in his wallet. I was a twenty-one-year-old emergency-room technician at the time when a young man in his early twenties was brought in, dead on arrival. He had been working on a construction job when a clutch failed on a large construction crane, and the crane had dropped a one-ton I beam on the young man below. He had no chance. As I looked in this stranger's wallet, I was very powerfully struck with a sense of personal identification. His wallet was very much like mine—a few dollars, a driver's license, a picture of a girl, and a few credit cards. Then it hit me. When he put the wallet in his pocket that morning, he had no idea that this is where he would be by the end of the day! I believe it was the first confrontation with my own mortality.

Why do we make these personal connections with the dead? What is it about a dead body that causes the kind of reactions we feel or need to feel as humans? One thing is becoming very clear. Viewing dead bodies and remains is an extreme stressor. In addition, it is as if our minds take a quick snapshot of the body, a snapshot that many of us do not want replayed. In the past most societies had more exposure to corpses than we do today. This fact may add to the emotional impact of the stressor. However, a growing amount of research suggests that some things trauma victims view are more stressful than others. The research of Ursano and Fullerton at the Uniformed Services University is suggesting a certain hierarchy of stressors. Dr. Fullerton has shared in briefings that viewing an intact body is less stressful than viewing a body part. Among body parts faces and hands are the most stressful. Among intact bodies viewing women is more stressful than men, and viewing babies and children is the most stressful. Putting the conclusions together, we could assume that viewing a decapitated baby or child would be the most stressful of all. These are extremely traumatic stressors for the viewer or the helper.[27]

Why are these things so damaging to the human psyche, and what do they say about us as humans? While working with Dr. Fullerton during a critical-incident stress course we were teaching together, I asked her why she thought viewing hands and faces was the most stressful. She replied that her research had brought her to the conclusion but she was not sure why. As I thought about my theological and biblical education, I made a connection in my mind. I told her it is interesting that these two human parts were the two most consistent ones used in anthropomorphic references to God in the Bible, that is, passages that describe God in human terms.

When Moses wanted to see God, God told him he could not view His face and live; therefore, Moses would have to be content with His back (see Ex. 33:18–23). The psalmist, asking for God's blessing on his life, prayed, "God be merciful to us and bless us,/And cause His face to shine upon us" (Ps. 67:1). When used of God, the face in biblical theology always expresses His essential personhood. The face is the symbol of personhood; it is the one part that represents the whole person. Therefore, it was not surprising to me that psychological researchers have concluded that our faces carry the essence of our personhood. Our faces reflect who we are to the world. When our faces are burned or mutilated, it is an extreme stressor. At that moment the well-meaning volunteer has become a victim and will probably need some special help.

But what about hands and fingers causes such an emotional response? Humans use their hands to greet each other. We work with our hands, we embrace with our hands, we spank our children with our hands, we even take care of ourselves with our hands. Without hands our livelihood, our affections, our ability to communicate and commune are severely handicapped. With our hands we embrace the world and involve ourselves in it. The same is true of God in biblical metaphors. God lifts up His hand to help the humble (see Ps. 10:12); with His hand people know about His works (see Ps. 28:4-5); His fatherly hand hangs on to His children (see Ps. 37:24); with His hand He pours out a cup of discipline (see Ps. 75:8); with His hands He fashioned the human race (see Ps. 119:73); the hand of God guided the affairs of the early church (see Acts 11:12) and led one Saul of Tarsus into the fold of Christendom (see Acts 13:11). The metaphor of the hand in the Bible expresses God's continuing involvement in the affairs of people, nations, and the church. His hand supports, guides, cares for, and disciplines.

Now we are faced with the chicken-and-egg question of which comes first. Is God like humankind, or is humankind like God? If one believes that humankind is made in the image of God, then it is reasonable to assume that these issues involving body parts are profoundly theological. The research is just discovering how God made us. Inherently, the knowledge that faces reflect the very nature of personhood and that hands represent all our involvement in life lies in the heart of every person. When we encounter these body parts dissociated or severely disfigured, it affects us deeply because it says the very image of God has been marred. That's why we turn our *faces* away from such sights. Our personhood cannot look at it long. What we feel is always at a much deeper level than we think because we are marvelously made by a wondrous Creator.

This chapter has concluded with the ugly side of trauma, but I hope that it has brought the reader closer to some issues rarely addressed in the general literature on the subject. My obvious bias is that many of the issues facing the field of trauma studies today are theological. I have not come to this conclusion because I was trained as a theologian. I can't remember any course in seminary that dealt distinctly with issues of trauma. I was backed into the position more and more through my personal experiences with the traumatized and my interaction with the mental-health community. It is my firm conviction that both the theologian and the trauma specialist need each other. I admit that I have only scratched the surface on the topics I have addressed and have missed many others that may need to be addressed. Both the theologian and the psychologist need to interact in dealing with these very important issues.

But for now the critical question emerges, especially in light of the severe types of stressors addressed in this chapter, when persons have either seen or done, or had done to them, the worst of all human events, can they ever be fully healed of the experience? In other words, once the scream has started, will it ever end?

The world breaks everyone,
then some become strong at the broken places.
Ernest Hemingway
A Farewell to Arms[1]

Wounds must be inspected and known
Must be kept open and probed and exposed to light.
Healing is from the bottom up
And from the outside in.
Marilyn McMahon
U.S. Navy Nurse Corps
Da Nang, Vietnam[2]

Blessed are those who mourn,
For they shall be comforted.
Matthew 5:4

CHAPTER 6

Will the Scream Ever End?

The bloody reign of Idi Amin deeply affected the lives of not only the Ugandan people but also the few Americans who stayed in the country for the sake of their vocations. One American businessman and his wife received a note stating that their twenty-six-year-old son had been kidnapped and was being held for ransom. The parents did nothing for a few days and then received a note threatening that their son would be killed if they did not pay the ransom. Government authorities advised them to resist payment. Then came another note. This was the final warning. If payment was not made immediately, their son would be tortured and killed. As they agonized over what to do, they received a note stating that their son was dead. The grief-stricken father tried to locate the body. Finally, he found someone who, for a price, would lead him to it. When he arrived at the appointed place, he was seized by a group of soldiers and taken to a prison. In the same cell that had held his son, they stripped him to the waist and made him face a wall. With a whip made of leather strips, they cut his back to ribbons. They loaded him onto the back of a pickup truck and dropped him off on a street corner. They shouted at him that if he ever tried to locate his son again, he would be killed. The father was unable to lie on his back for two months. Two years later, this couple had suffered bitter, deep hatred toward the soldiers who murdered their son. They could no longer enjoy success in business, their home in the country, or a happy family life. Each day was filled with sorrow, hatred, and thoughts of revenge.[3]

What kind of help is there for a couple that have experienced what they did? It would seem that they had every right to their bitterness, hatred, and thoughts of revenge. No one would debate that. However, the important question to ask is, "Do you want to live the rest of your life this way?" If the answer is no, then how does one move from being a victim to a survivor? Will this couple finally reach a point when the pain of their son's death and the psychic memory of being tortured lose their power? To answer these questions is to strike at the heart of the recovery movement today.

If recovery from such ordeals is possible, then how does it come about, and what does recovery involve? That will be the focus of this chapter. To understand properly what recovery looks like, it is first imperative to talk about the nature of psychic pain.

What Is Psychic Pain?

In preparation for writing this chapter, I examined almost everything I could find in libraries and bookstores on the subjects of inner healing (Payne), healing of memories (Seamands), healing of adult children of alcoholics (Woilitz, Kritsberg), and the popular literature on healing the inner child (Bradshaw). When I came to this particular section, I needed a concise definition of what I have been calling psychic pain. However, I was disappointed to find that in the abundance of literature listed in the endnotes, a clear definition of such a concept was not found. Therefore, I will offer my own. Psychic pain is what we feel in response to being wounded by traumatic events.

Personally, I think that limiting the pain we bear as adults to what we have suffered in childhood does not do justice to the continued wounding that many of us face throughout our adult lives. A man may not have been raised in a dysfunctional family, or a woman may not have been sexually abused by her father, but each still may be profoundly wounded by traumatic events as an adult. In these cases there is just as much need for healing adult pain as there is for healing childhood pain. Pain is pain, no matter how it got there. As one Vietnam veteran expressed it, "I was too young when I went . . . and too old when I got home." The pain he bears is not the pain from his inner child but the pain of having been wounded by the loss of his late adolescence and early adulthood. This is psychic pain because it is rooted in his psyche, the depth of

145

his soul, imbedded in his human spirit called the self . . . the person he was and is.

Psychic pain is the pain we feel when our personhood has been attacked and wounded. The pain does not seemingly go away with time; therefore, psychic pain is an abiding pain. The mother who loses a child still has the empty space in her heart. The ache is her psychic pain. The HIV-positive patient who may not have developed full-blown AIDS yet is a carrier of far more than a deadly virus. He also carries psychic pain every day. Even though he feels fine when he wakes up in the morning, with the awakening of consciousness the sting of psychic pain also greets him with his morning coffee. Divorced men and women may go throughout their day looking as if all is well, but from my experience in doing divorce-recovery workshops (Fresh Start Seminars, Inc.), I know that most carry significant psychic pain.

Psychic pain results from memories we cannot get rid of. But why do we remember what we remember? Why can we forget very easily the things we were supposed to learn in school? I hate it when my kids ask me for help in their algebra or geometry assignments. I remember that I took the subjects, but I don't have a clue in solving the problems. I know that I once could, but now I can't. But take traumatic stress. I don't even consciously have to say to myself, *I want to remember this because this is having such an impact on me.* In some cases in which onlookers who observe car accidents or other disasters just glance out of the corner of their eyes and see mutilated people, this is enough to ingrain the picture in their minds permanently. Why is this true?

How Memories Are Stored: the Brain

It's fairly obvious that the brain stores these negative images very quickly somewhere. After the Judge Thomas and Anita Hill hearings even *Time* devoted a major article to the issue of whether our memories can be trusted.[4] The issue in the whole "trial" was the issue of memory. Dr. Richard Restak, a well-published neurologist, has discussed how stressful situations stimulate our brains to produce amounts of noradrenaline. The release of noradrenaline into our bloodstreams when under extreme stress expands our general awareness capability. Adrenaline produces the fight-or-flight response through the introduction of the hormone into the bloodstream. Restak wrote, "Neuroscientists now believe that noradrenaline plays an important role in our general awareness. We tend to notice and remember events that occur when we are most alert and responsive to our environment—i.e., when our arousal level is at its peak." He went on to say that when a rat is given electric shock and adrenaline is injected into the rat, its "memory" is heightened concerning the shock. Restak concluded, "The adrenaline heightens the rat's level of arousal, makes it more susceptible to the unpleasant effects of the electric shock. It also may open the gates of memory so that particular events are more likely to be recalled. A trivial event, in short, is transformed into a meaningful and significant one."[5]

Consider what happens in a car accident or to the Desert Storm veteran. After an accident the fear and shock that an individual feels as he is lying in the seat of a smashed car causes the brain to produce increased amounts of adrenaline. The increase of adrenaline expands the awareness level psychologically, which allows for all the sights, sounds, and smells to be recorded more effectively in the mind. In the sands of Iraq, as the soldier storms into an Iraqi bunker, his heart is pounding, and he doesn't know what he will find when he goes into the enemy bunker. Will it be empty? Will the soldiers immediately put up their hands and become POWs, or will they open fire on the intruders? The adrenaline rush enlarges the emotional side of the situation and makes it more memorable and volatile than it really may be. Then, when a buddy hits a booby trap that blows off his arm, the tragedy is recorded once for all with such vivid imagery that when the veteran returns home, he continues to dream about the action. Even a similar sight or smell can bring back the realism of that traumatic moment in the sand. The scream is not only a videotape but also a replay of the entire emotional experience.

So, if psychic pain is what we feel in response to the wounds we have received, and because of the adrenaline rush of the moment the complete sight and sound show of the trauma has been recorded in our mental computers, is it ever possible to erase these painful images? Is healing possible? First, we need to talk about the nature of healing. The term, as used, if not overused, today, has taken on meanings that make it even more difficult to understand. It is used for everything and anything. From the healing of our bodies to the healing of our inner child, the term is used as if everyone knows what healing should look like.

What Is Healing?

The process by which the recording of painful memories takes place is not totally understood. We can remember

148

some things but not necessarily with the same intensity as when they first happened. Restak has pointed out:

Although it is easy to recall events from our childhood, particularly if we are cued by a family photograph album, it is a lot harder to evoke the emotions that accompanied the events. I have a picture of myself at age twelve on the occasion of receiving my first bicycle. Although I remember this as one of the happiest days of my childhood, I can't summon up the feelings I had at the time. To do so, it would probably be necessary to see the bike once again, perhaps even sit on it, or somehow re-create as many of the sensory aspects of that occasion as possible. "For reasons we don't understand, the emotions involved are often far less accessible to our memories than the images we have stored for events in our past," points out Dr. Mishkin.

It is likely that differences exist in people's abilities to reexperience their emotional memories. Creativity, especially the evocative genius of a Proust, may depend on a heightened ability to "get in touch" with the emotions and not just the images of the past. The flip side of this ability may involve painful, haunting memories that can't be forgotten despite strongest efforts. Such memories torture severely depressed patients, sometimes to the point of suicide—they are memories gone awry, memories that seem to have taken on a malevolent life of their own.

In everyday life, memories are also formed in relation to emotionally upsetting events. Can you recall where you were when President Kennedy was shot? Most people who in 1963 were adolescents or older can vividly recall today what they were doing when they first heard that the President was shot. These "flashbulb" memories, as they are called, are sharply etched within our minds because they involve a sudden upheaval of powerful emotions: shock, pity, anger, disbelief, outrage. Does this mean that "flashbulb" memories are encoded within the brain in different ways from memories of ordinary events? This is almost certainly the case. . . . All this may suggest that our memories are dependent on our capacities for the more profound emotions: to be shocked, to care, to experience life with vividness and intensity. In any case, this relationship of memory to emotion surely is more than fortuitous. We remember best those events that had an emotional impact on us, unless, of course, the events were too upsetting (causing the memory to shut down due to too much adrenaline).[6]

In the high-energy, adrenaline-filled moments when our most traumatic events take place, the flashbulbs went off, capturing the moment in the mind's eye. It's still there, like old photos reminding us of the pain, sometimes with even the same emotional intensity. Today there is a host of "cures" for such things. The range of healings available today is limited only by the therapists who publicize their cures. As I have read about or have been exposed to these approaches, I have always come away with many new, helpful insights and approaches for my own life and work. However, at the same time, I also come away with a profound sense that something is still lacking. I find myself wondering if the reality equals the promise. Sometimes merely believing in the promise is the cure; "I believe I am healed; therefore, I am." Personally, I think our faith in the human ability to bring about complex internal changes has been grossly overrated. One researcher had the courage to do a large-scale evaluation of the entire mental-health community and its claims about psychological change. Dr. Zilbergeld, a clinical psychologist, stated:

Our culture is strongly committed to the proposition that people are highly malleable [changeable]. Three key assumptions of the present age are that human beings should change because they are not as competent or as good or as happy as they could be; that there are few limits to the alterations they can make; and that change is relatively easy to effect. If only the right methods are used and the right attitudes are held, people can make significant changes and become almost whatever they want.[7]

Dr. Zilbergeld went on to point out that America has always been a society deeply committed to utopian ideals and snake-oil promises. In the last chapter of his book he tried to put his own profession in perspective by looking at the realism of change. He wrote:

The limits of personal change discussed so far become less depressing and easier to accept with the realization that there is far less reason for changing ourselves than we have been led to believe, and that there are advantages to not trying to improve ourselves. . . . We are not nearly as bad off and in need of fixing as therapists tell us. Much of what we now think of as problems—things that ought to be altered and for which there are solutions—are not so much problems as inescapable limits and predicaments of life. We see them as problems only because we have developed peculiar notions about what life can and should be. Putting these things in perspective, seeing them as inherent in the structure of life rather than as problems we can solve, will not make them go away but may allow us to avoid the dangers of pursuing unrealistic expectations and the self-criticism that so often accompanies failure to change. . . . A lot of what we now call problems and want to get rid of are what make people interesting. That the great captain of industry is afraid of dogs or airplanes, that the strong man or woman is obsessed by fear of failure, that someone who appears to have it all together feels confused most of the time or can't get much of anything together in the bedroom, that the preacher of positive thinking is often depressed, that some

151

great changers of others can't change themselves—these "flaws" are often what make them appealing, more human, and draw us to them. Many of these people would be far less interesting and attractive without their problems. . . . Not knowing what else to do, we try to change ourselves and eliminate the feelings.[8]

Don't read the good doctor wrong. He is not against counseling or psychotherapy. He would be out of a career if he were! What he is against is the prevailing assumption that everything can be fixed, cured, or healed. In fact, he says, perhaps it's time to do the proper reframing and see our problems as aspects of who we really are and what makes us unique, interesting individuals. A man who has made a major contribution to my life is just such a man. I've always called him a "one-trick pony." He does one thing well . . . very well. Years ago he was smart enough to build his whole career on it. The rest of his life is a mess. What's really funny is that he doesn't even have enough self-perception to see it. Is this denial or not wanting to face reality? No, I don't think so. I believe he is very much in touch with reality. He has also wrestled with depression all his life. Once he told me, "I am a depressive personality. That's how I view the world when I am really me." I would agree with Zilbergeld—these are the quirks that make my friend interesting. I hope he stays the way he is!

I have said all this at the front end only to try to put the issue of psychic healing into perspective. I believe change and healing are possible, but they are not as easy as often touted. Besides, there are some things we may have to learn to live with, but the good news is that we *can* learn to live with them. To me this is far more in keeping with reality while also suggesting that healing is possible.

As I mentioned earlier, there are many options for healing today, all of which may offer something of value for releasing the yet unscreamed screams of the traumatized. What are some of these options?

Healing by Uncovering:
Getting Naked before Others

This approach probably has its roots in the father of all therapy, Sigmund Freud. We all have very sophisticated strategies for deceiving ourselves and others in order to cope with the realities of the pain we bear. These defense mechanisms are very common and function adequately, for the most part, until something comes along our path that we can't handle. In trauma we may keep denying the pain, or remain angry, or spend the rest of our lives trying to cut little deals with God in order to keep from really looking at our pain and seeing the hidden messages in it. The goal in therapy is, then, to get all the stuff out, sometimes in the presence of others who share the same kind of pain. It's a "Let's get naked together" kind of experience. The assumption is that once we have exposed all the hidden devices we all use to cover our pain and own up to these strategies, healing should take place. Again, I believe this approach *can* be effective for some people who need this kind of fairly gutsy examination and exposure. However, my concern is for what happens after everyone has all his emotional clothes off! Are we merely calling nakedness healing and wellness? Sometimes it strikes me that we may be playing "The Emperor's New Clothes" game. We all think we are well dressed because we are wearing invisible clothes. The reality is, we are just naked. Becoming vulnerable about my pain and learning how I have used various strategies in my life to deny or manage that pain may be helpful in moving me toward healing. But just because I have all my self-deceptive strategies out on the table doesn't mean I am well or healed. Healing goes much further.[9]

My concern is for what I see as a growing tendency to define wellness by sickness. I have heard on the streets of our culture statements like "All of us are sick or dysfunctional" or "I don't trust anyone who didn't come from a dysfunctional family." Most of our TV sitcoms today portray the dysfunctional family as the "normal" family ("Married with Children," "The Simpsons"). Oprah, Sally, and Geraldo give us daily doses of dysfunction with the most ridiculous themes. The result is an attempt to normalize even the most bizarre deviations. Even the very popular Bradshaw series on the family, which is being aired all over the country, comes very close to suggesting that dysfunction today is normative. Even if it is statistically normative (more than 50 percent of the families in America are dysfunctional), this does not make it the standard of wellness. If over 50 percent of our population had cancer, I don't believe the medical profession would say that having cancer is what makes one well. That would be irresponsible, making sickness the equivalent of wellness. A truly dysfunctional person is one who can't function at all! This is the person we commit to psychiatric wards because he can no longer care for himself or has become a danger to himself or others.[10] Today some of these examples are being touted as paradigms of a new psychological wellness. This deeply concerns me because it is potentially dangerous. Most of the individuals I know who have come from dysfunctional families still get to work everyday and manage most of their lives relatively well. Often what brings them into counseling is an area in which the dysfunctional baggage is causing them pain. But I would still consider them reasonably well people.

Healing by Finding and Talking to the Inner Child

The concept of the inner child is not new, but it has become increasingly popular. From Freud to Erikson, Horney and Sullivan, all have talked much about the child within.[11] The child within is the real or true self who has never had the freedom to develop properly. It is the part of us that is ultimately alive, energetic, creative, and fulfilled but that has been put down by parents, institutions, education, religion, politics, the media, or significant early-childhood trauma.[12] The theoretical aspects of the concept are sound. As children, we need freedom, love, acceptance, and a nurturing environment in which to grow to maturity. When this environment is not present, the child remains a child even when he is grown. Adults whose inner child has not developed lack natural zest for freedom and creative expression and function merely as codependents. They are always trying to please others, being out of touch with their feelings or not even knowing if they have feelings. For incest or rape victims, the child within has been drastically harmed and buried by emotional denial. During rape or incest the child splits with himself and the reality that is taking place. This split creates a dualism within the person.[13] For healing to take place, we as adult children must find the child that was lost and harmed and become reunited with it.

Some therapeutic techniques that have been found to be helpful are those John Bradshaw has popularized. In order to "heal the shame that binds," he encourages the victim to heal the memories by reestablishing contact with the child within, even talking to it. Bradshaw explains, "This is done by simply closing your eyes and letting your memory take you back to a time when Mom or Dad or a teacher or preacher was laying their shame on you." Having called up this memory, you then "close your eyes and think of a time when you were being articulate. The memory can come from any time in your life. You are speaking firmly and clearly, saying exactly what you want to say."[14] As you carry on this conversation with your inner child, a certain restructuring of the old memory is supposed to take place.[15] It is a sort of reconditioning of the painful moment by folding over it a memory in which you were brilliant in your counteroffensive against your parents, preacher, teacher, or attacker. Associated with this exercise are relaxation techniques and reprogramming of the old tapes (voices) from the hostile past. I know many who have been extremely helped by these exercises and are greatly appreciative of Bradshaw's bringing to the forefront the concept of inner shame that literally keeps many in bondage.[16]

I also know of veterans who, no matter how often they try to identify and talk to their "inner-older child" who got wounded in Vietnam, are unable to heal. In these men there are no positive memories of Vietnam to erase or cover the horror they experienced. In their personal histories there are no memories of brilliance in which they did the right thing. Picturing Vietnam with beautiful flowers and ocean breezes does not erase the horror of the experience. Or instead of killing and mutilating an enemy, he shakes hands with him, embraces him, and shares family photos. These are not in the memory bank of actuality for most veterans. They are pure fantasy, and fantasy will never bring healing. I believe some deeply moral and emotional issues are left untouched and unhealed by this method. Although I appreciate some of Bradshaw's work, I'm not sure his methods can deal with the moral implications of traumatic events or acknowledge any relevance to moral discussion.[17]

I should also say that I believe these concepts are very helpful for those who have been reared in dysfunctional families and never thought about the pain that may be buried because they were never allowed to experience their pain in the family. But the method should not be used as a universal theoretical base for dealing with posttraumatic stress of the more critical-incident type (rape, incest, war, air crashes, and so on).

Another popular branch of the inner-healing movement is what I would designate the spiritual-healing-of-memories school.

Spiritual Healing of Memories

Spiritual-healing practitioners utilize prayer, mixed with relaxation techniques and visualization on the person of Jesus. David Seamands, in his best-selling volume *Healing of Memories*, talks about how to conduct one of these prayer sessions.

Begin by explaining or reminding the counselee about the concepts of prayer which are basic to memory healing. Remind him or her that Jesus Christ is Lord and, therefore, the Lord of time. Describe how Jesus will be walking back into time with you and dealing with the situation as He would have, had you asked Him at the time. Once more clarify the reason for this—"the real problems are not with the adult, the grown-up person you are just now. So we need to reach back into the past and let Jesus deal with your child in those places which need the actual healing. This is because you seem to be stuck or hung up at those particular places of hurt. So far as possible, I want you to talk to God as if you are now the child (or young person or adult) you were at that hurting place in your life." [18]

Another Christian writer offers an eight-step progression that is supposed to lead toward the healing of memories.

Step 1: Recall a time when you were hurt.
Step 2: Write out all that you can remember about the event. What happened? What were your feelings? What did you do? What thoughts ran through your head? What conclusions did you draw from the event?
Step 3: Decide what you needed at the time. We cannot change the behavior of others. What happened to us is a fact. But we did need something we did not get. Usually protection, comfort, safety, positive statements, and meaningful touches were missing. Whatever it was, record it.
Step 4: Sit down in a comfortable chair or lie down. Plan for a few minutes to be alone.

. . . .

Step 6: Picture the scene. Use the notes you've written to fully imagine the event.
Step 7: Bring into your scene your image of God or Christ. Make Him as real as you can. Have Him give to you what you needed. Perhaps it is a hug. Have Him do it. Or maybe you needed to hear you are OK and not to blame for the actions of your parent. Have Him tell you. Perhaps you needed to know this hurt will be healed, stopped or make sense some day. Have Him give you whatever gift you need. Hold the image as long as you need. His very presence is healing.

Step 8: End the time with a prayer, thanking Him for His presence and asking Him for direction to guide your needs.[19]

The author then outlines a new process whereby the client can begin to interrupt and replace the unpleasant thoughts with healthier ones. One can easily see the similarity between Bradshaw's healing of the inner child and this spiritual-healing approach. The technique is largely the same, but the content differs. Both help the individual relax and then begin the process of visualizing and replacing the traumatic experience with more positive imagery. The one above in particular focuses on having Jesus meet, in mystical fashion, the unmet needs of one's childhood. Again, I have known some for whom this visualization provided a needed corrective to the pain of their memories. Whether it is what I would call healing, I'm not sure yet.

Two brother Jesuits have used Kubler-Ross's stages of grief as a theoretical model from which to bring about this spiritual healing. They wrote:

> In healing memory we do the same with the Lord. We take Him by the hand and go back to a hurt we don't want to see.... Healing a memory drains out our old fears and feelings and pours in Christ's feelings when we take His hand.... This is the same struggle with of denial, anger, bargaining, and depression that the dying experience in forgiving God, others, and themselves for their declining life.[20]

Through prayer and visualization they encourage the traumatized to use Jesus as their loving guide, taking them by the hand back through their experience. Their focus is on both offering and receiving forgiveness in every critical trauma.

Another name in the spiritual-healing category is Leanne Payne, who has become known throughout the world for her emphasis on the role of prayer in healing. Although her approach has some points in common with the above techniques, it is more centered on the reality of the divine presence and on how the crucifixion and resurrection of Jesus relate to the healing of memories. She believes "the power to heal and to be healed is available because God Himself is in our midst. His Presence and His power are mysteriously one and we who live and move and have our being in God are called to preach, teach and heal in that spiritual power and authority."[21] She utilizes dream interpretation to identify hidden inner pain and then invokes the divine presence to heal the inner recesses of the psyche. Her ministry is one of prayer and illumination, whereby the person can begin to walk in this divine presence, the source of true healing.[22] She also strongly emphasizes each person's making the connection between his own pain and the pain of Christ on the cross. She explains:

> To sum up, then, Christ is the Healer. We do not take another's suffering, sin, or sickness into or upon ourselves. This Christ has already done—in Gethsemane and on the Cross. We point always to the One who cried out on the Cross, "My God, my God, why hast thou forsaken me?" We yield up to Him alone our suffering and our sin. In exchange, He then imparts life and healing.[23]

You can see the range of perspectives available on this subject today. I have only scratched the surface of the available literature and probably have not done justice to the views listed. I have tried to give you a flavor of developments in this movement. As I said before, all of these have helped individuals and have received their own praise.

My personal feeling about therapy techniques is that we often have in this field an application of the Hawthorne effect. The Hawthorne study was one of the first research attempts to find out what makes employees work better and more effectively. The assumption of the study was that better lighting would produce a happier work force, which in turn would increase production. Therefore, the researchers increased the wattage of lights, put in more lights, and opened up the workplace to allow more natural light. The result? Employees reported greater happiness, and production went up. The assumption was correct! Well, maybe. The researchers felt they should be more positive about the results before drawing any real conclusions. So they did another study in which they lowered the wattage, reduced the number of lights, and obstructed the natural light of windows. The result? Employees reported increased happiness with the workplace, and production went up. The researchers couldn't believe their results. In further studies they changed the work environment in as many ways as they could, but no matter what they did, production went up, and employees reported high satisfaction.

What has now commonly become known as the Hawthorne effect is that what produced the happiness and the consequent high level of production was something they weren't even studying. It was so much a part of the method that they couldn't recognize it. What was it? After every change in the environment the workers were asked what they thought about the changes and how they were affected by them. As a result, the workers felt valued. They appreciated the fact that they were being asked about their work and that their input was being given serious attention. The study had empowered them, making them feel a part of the operation of the company. As a result, they were happy no matter how much light they had to work in, and their production levels revealed their satisfaction.

I see the same dynamic in counseling. The best methods in the hands of an uncaring professional will probably not accomplish much healing. Even the worst methods in the hands of someone caring, accepting, and granting the value of personhood to the traumatized will accomplish much. It is always humbling to realize this. Often someone with fewer professional credentials or less training has a more prosperous practice simply because she becomes known throughout a community as one who cares and listens!

So far I have outlined the views of others on the subject of healing. As I conclude this section, I need to articulate what I see as the most important aspects of healing. But first let me give my own definition of healing.

A Definition of Healing for the Traumatized

Healing means different things to different people. As I study the research and work with those who have met with tough events in life, these are the conclusions about healing I have reached at this point.

I define healing as a new way of seeing, a new way of feeling, and a new way of living. With this definition it is, then, the goal of the therapist, friend, spouse, or parent to help the individual work toward grasping this sense of newness. The definition assumes that healing is a process of undesignated time duration. Some may heal quicker than others, some may heal relatively completely, and some never. But this does not mean the end of the world. As mentioned earlier, posttraumatic-stress disorder is something that individuals can live with. A person who has not been completely healed is not a sick individual. He or she still has normal reactions to abnormal events. For what they have been through, they are behaving normally, even though they are not totally restored to pretrauma functioning. The above definition also reflects a holistic observation about healing. Healing is more than the healing of memories or the healing of the inner child. It has to do with becoming a whole person. Being a whole person involves having a purpose for living and how one views life.

Being whole also means having our range of feelings expanded. I believe it has taken some of my mid-life trauma for me to begin experiencing a broader range of emotions. One emotion I have discovered has seriously scared me. I've always been a sort of low-key personality until I hit the stressors and changes of mid-life. What I have discovered through much pain is my inner rage at many things. I hope that this emotional door will widen my range not only on the negative side but also on the positive side so I can also begin to experience a greater degree of joy and excitement. A whole person can experience the full range of available human emotions.[24] Whether it is because of traumatic events, or our conformist educational systems, or certain religious doctrines, or accepting the standards of our company, most of us are never allowed to experience the full range of our emotional capabilities.

Healing also means a new way of living. Living involves relationships. The traumatized, in order to survive, have closed inside themselves. Healing means opening again to other people; restoring relationships that have been broken, harmed, or wronged; and even restoring a lost relationship with God.

Perhaps at this point it might be helpful to say that I see psychic healing as very similar to the medical healing that physicians do. Between my junior and senior years of college, I worked as a surgery technician in a metropolitan hospital. I learned all the surgical instruments and scrubbed in on almost every conceivable type of surgery, both minor and serious. I still remember the impact one brilliant neurosurgeon made on me as a young college student. Many doctors in the hospital did not necessarily have the best reputations. But I had always heard nothing but praise for this particular physician. He was a Harvard graduate and had done his residency at Mayo Clinic. I was excited when I saw my name listed to assist him in a brain-tumor removal. During surgery he talked to me, asked me about my plans, and at the end of the operation asked if he could teach me anything about the brain. I asked, "What causes the brain to develop tumors?" He answered, "I don't know." Then I asked, "How does healing take place after we put the piece of skull back in place?" He laughed. "Listen," he said, "all I do here is take out the pieces of the brain that have died, and then God does the healing. I just cooperate with the laws God has built into the human system." What a lesson from a humble yet brilliant man! I believe it is the same for psychic healing. We probably know more about what does not facilitate healing than what really does. My conclusion is very similar to the neuro-surgeon's. We must cooperate with the laws that God has already ordained for proper human functioning. We are not the healers, but we can cooperate with the healing process. This is the combination of both active and passive processes.

Healing in the Middle Voice

I always knew there would be a use for all the Greek I was forced to take in seminary. Given enough time, I could at least use something from it as an illustration for something else. So here it is right in the context of healing. I must admit that the idea is not original with me. An article by Eugene Peterson first brought it to my attention, but John White applied it to the present subject for me.[25]

In the English language we do not have a middle voice. We get by with the two voices of active and passive. For those who wonder what in the world this means, let me illustrate. If I say, "I bathed my child," that's active voice. I was doing the bathing for someone else. If I say, "I was bathed by my child," that's passive voice. I received the bath from outside myself by the hand of someone else. But if I say, "I bathed myself," this is the closest expression we have in English of the Greek middle voice.[26] It expresses that I am both the subject doing the action, at the same time being acted upon. (The water is coming from outside on me.) Basically, I am both the performer and receiver of the action. I believe this is the precise analogy my neurosurgeon friend was explaining to me. He was both the performer of the actions that would bring about healing, yet he was also the receiver. God was ultimately the healer who, through the marvelous laws of bodily functioning, would bring about the healing.

I prefer to view psychic healing the same way. We are performers of certain actions that can lead to healing, but we are also receivers of healing that is outside, involving agents that are beyond us. I can do some things to facilitate my own healing, but I should never start believing that because I am doing all the things I am supposed to do, healing should be the result. Healing is more than what I do for myself. Healing is also more than what other counselors, therapists, friends, and family can do. I am convinced more than ever that when we talk about healing, we are talking about something that is very mysterious, if not mystical. It is the human spirit that has been wounded in trauma. To facilitate healing in the deepest parts of the unconscious as well as the conscious, we must make contact with this spirit. It takes a spirit to make contact with spirit. Jesus had great insight into human and divine psychology when He said, "That which is born of the flesh is flesh, and that which is born of the Spirit is spirit" (John 3:6). If man is not only a material being (flesh) but also a spiritual being, then contact must be made with the Spirit of God in order to have true healing. As noted earlier, the alienation and abandonment the victim feels as a result of the trauma are total. The victim feels all alone in his pain (alienation). Compared to the rest of the world, he now feels like an alien. Many Vietnam veterans describe their first experience of homecoming precisely in those terms. They came home to an alien nation, one they no longer knew and one that no longer wanted them. But they also felt alienated from God. Where was God in Vietnam? God could not have been there. Therefore, the second feeling is even greater. The victim comes to the conclusion that everyone has abandoned or will abandon him. People really don't understand what the raped woman, or the air-crash victim, or the HIV-positive patient is experiencing. Consequently, even though they may be around people all day and have people in their lives who care deeply for them, they often feel abandoned.

If my definition of healing is accurate, then what will cause a person to *want* to see, feel, and act differently? I say *want* because all healing must begin with the desire to be different. I remember reading the New Testament for the first time in college and being surprised when Jesus actually asked a man who had been ill for thirty-eight years if he wanted to get well (see John 5:5–6). It struck me as funny to ask a man such a question. Of course, the man would want to get well. But after some twenty years of working with people with all kinds of problems, I now see the question differently. Jesus revealed what almost any counselor has had to find out through much frustration and patience. Many hurting people do not want to get well. They have so learned to see themselves as victims of terrible circumstances that once anyone moves in to help them, they either back off or sabotage the efforts. They are not ready yet. They don't want to be different. Healing begins with the *desire* for change.

Healing as Change

With the publication of my first book, *Uneasy Manhood*, I had the opportunity to do the book tour and radio call-in circuit. Talking about men's issues in our culture always gets one into trouble if you talk long enough. On most radio call-in shows, sooner if not later, a woman will call in and ask, "What can I do to get my husband to do or be ... ?" My answer is never well received. I simply say, "I think the only thing you *can* do is to give up the idea that there is something you *can* do to change your husband." The same applies to healing. As Dr. Zilbergeld stated earlier in the chapter, we just assume that change is not only possible but also easy. A related assumption also dominates much thinking about psychological change. It is assumed that we can change ourselves by merely intentioning such. I certainly believe that human beings are capable of changing, but I don't necessarily believe that the changes are intentional. Most significant changes are the results of other things. Remember the Hawthorne effect? What the traumatic-stress victim must bring to his own healing is a willingness for something to happen within him. He wants to move from his alienation and abandonment toward a newer and fresher sense of wholeness and community. What, then, are some active steps the victim can take to begin the process?

What makes us in any relationship want to see, feel, and do something differently? Usually, it is a relationship with a person. Over the years my wife and my kids have been able to get me to do all kinds of things that I wasn't too excited about doing. How? By nagging, demanding, or threatening? No, by their loving presence and involvement in my life. Healing then begins with either the first encounter with an ultimate Person or a return to the Person who got lost in our pain.

The Healing Nature of Presence

In chapter 5 I tried to show that many issues in this field of trauma raise questions that are rooted in theology. Theology has to do with God and His relations with the world—that includes us. This being the case, our difficulty in healing also has to do with God. Whether or not we like it, whether or not we are sincerely religious, it really doesn't matter. When traumatic events happen to us, we make the connection very quickly that if there is a God, our pain could have been prevented. Somehow we instinctively connect with Him and blame Him through the pain of our trauma. Deep down we are angry at Him, even though we aren't quite sure who He is. The best start for being an active agent in our own healing is to come back to a realization of His presence. The only cure for our feelings of alienation and abandonment is presence . . . divine presence. This presence is universal over all creation.

The Creator's Presence

We are all born into the family of humankind. I am of the persuasion that humankind did not just happen. Our universe reflects a purposeful Creator. When we look at humankind, we see this marvelous creation, which, the Bible says, is made "in the image of God" (Gen. 1:27). As creatures made in God's image, we are all fellow brothers and sisters in the human race. We share creaturely concerns, hopes, fears, and pains. Since the Enlightenment it has not been "intellectually correct" to believe in a God who also shares these human concerns. With the Enlightenment, even if someone believed in God, He was viewed as sort of an absent watchmaker who, after creating it, wound it up, sold it, and now has no more relationship to it. Therefore, this God, if He is there at all, is irrelevant to human pain and can do nothing about its cure. Today, with New Age thinking dominating the streets, it has gotten even worse. God is whatever or whoever one wants. The classic distinction between God and humankind is removed, and man now becomes his own god, merged into a monistic (everything is one) reality. In this thinking, God is found by turning within and finding oneself, making the person divine in his own right. Obviously, then, this is not a god who is external to the person and who can bring healing from the outside. If there is healing, it depends on my finding and healing myself.

The classic Judeo-Christian teaching has been that God is both outside His creation (transcendence) *and* within His creation (immanence) at the same time. I find many Christians today who believe both of these but who have never thought about the implications of His immanence for the subject of healing. Immanence means that God's presence is really in all that we do and in all that has happened to us. The same King David who often accused God of not doing anything to remove the evil around him (see Ps. 22:1–2) also held to this sustaining, universal presence in his pain. He articulated:

Where can I go from Your Spirit?
Or where can I flee from Your presence?
If I ascend into heaven, You are there;
If I make my bed in hell, behold, You are there. . . .
Indeed, the darkness shall not hide from You,
But the night shines as the day;
The darkness and the light are both alike to You
(Ps. 139:7–8, 12).

He even went on to point out that while we were being knit together in our mother's womb, God's presence was there as well.

Yes, the biblical writers had an assumption about God. They believed that He was really there, even in the midst of His people's pain. We find such expressions as God's being grieved (see Gen. 6:6), God's hearing His people's groaning and knowing their sorrows (see Ex. 2:24, 3:7), God's bearing misery (see Judg. 10:16), God's yearning (see Jer. 31:20), God's heart churning within Him in regard to His people (see Hos. 11:8). In a startling passage the prophet Isaiah said, "In all their affliction He was afflicted" (Isa. 63:9). The perspective of the biblical writers was that God really feels, and He feels the pain of His people. If Jesus is accepted as the God-Man, who fully demonstrates what God is like (see John 1:14, 18; 14:7, 10), this same portrait of a feeling God is presented. Jesus grieved and wept over the condition of His people (see Matt. 23:37–39); He felt compassion for the sick and afflicted (see Matt. 20:34); He is called Immanuel, Hebrew for "God with us" (see Matt. 1:23); and He taught that when one mistreats the poor, the naked, the sick, and the stranger, one, in fact, is mistreating Him (see Matt. 25:41–45). In the biblical writers' minds there was a connection between what we as humans feel and what God feels.

At this point I must express what has been a long-standing difficulty with biblical language. In some circles these expressions have merely been written off as anthropomorphisms (human terms or language). What this means is that the biblical writers, in attempting to articulate what God is like, could use only human terms and language to express such qualities as God's concern for His people. The implication is that God does not *really* feel, grieve, or hurt with His creation. He is in reality a nonpassionate and incapable-of-feeling deity. He does not feel what humankind feels. This, unfortunately, has colored much about how we feel toward God. In response to this "passivity" of God the Anglican scholar John Stott has written:

> It is true that Old Testament language is an accommodation to our human understanding, and that God is represented as experiencing human emotion. Yet, to acknowledge that His feelings are not human is not to deny that they are real. If they are only metaphorical, then the only God left to us will be the infinite iceberg of metaphysics ... The frequent anthropopathisms (which ascribe human suffering to God) are not to be

rejected as crude or primitive, but rather to be welcomed as crucial to our understanding of him.[27]

Later in the same book Stott concluded, "Were God incapable of suffering . . . , then He would also be incapable of love, whereas the one who is capable of love is also capable of suffering for he also opens himself to the suffering which is involved in love."[28]

In my opinion, the first step in realizing healing from our psychic pain is to recognize that God was really present when the tragedy occurred. Even though I may feel that He was absent, He was very much there, grieving, hurting, and perhaps even being angered by the injustice of it. God does not lead a sheltered life, as some think. His universal presence extends to the worst of events. God was in Vietnam, He was at the Holocaust, He was at the rape scene, He was there when a child died. He is still here. We cannot flee from His presence even when we try. As one griever told me, "I found that I ran right into Him when I was running away." Healing begins in His presence. It is in His presence that new reconstructive emotions (joy and pleasure) have their origins (see Ps. 16:11). These emotions must come from the conviction that Someone cares deeply about me and knows exactly what I have experienced because He was there in the trauma. In this sense, the first thing we can do for our healing is to return to God.

Once a teenage girl, after graduating from high school, felt oppressed by her parents and was tired of trying to live up to the image created by her older sister. Her father had been a good financial planner from the time of her birth, so a nice college fund had been set aside. But she had other ideas. She wasn't interested in pursuing a college education, so she asked her dad if she could take her college money and instead go to California, get an apartment, and figure out what she wanted to do with her life. The father thought it unwise, but he cared deeply for his daughter and had always tried to do the right thing for her. The girl's perception of her dad was different. She viewed him as distant and unfair. The father, realizing that his daughter was old enough to leave if she wanted to, finally agreed to cashing out of the college fund and sending her on her way. He embraced her and watched with a tear in his eye as his daughter drove off toward the West.

The atmosphere in the car was far different. Hopes of a movie career or meeting Mr. Right made her heart beat faster as she drove off. She thought of the fun in the sun, the type of apartment she would have, and the people she would meet. When she arrived, it was better than she ever dreamed. The beaches were unbelievable, much more beautiful than the Jersey shore she had grown up with. The guys were all friendly and so attractive. She found a lovely apartment and began furnishing it. Some roommates soon followed, and it seemed that her new life was off and running. But her apartment cost far more than she had expected, and she found herself paying fees to everyone who promised to make her famous. She took acting lessons and got an agent; there were résumé and portfolio fees. Money was going out, but none was coming in. The attractive guys who were so friendly also took advantage of her. Her roommates weren't carrying their load on the phone and energy bills. Every morning when she woke up, there were different guys and beer cans all over the place. Finally, the worst thing happened that could ever happen to a young southern-California expectant starlet. She ran out of money and had to look for a job! Jobs in LA were hard enough to find for the well trained and educated. For someone with no college or work experience, things were even worse. Then the recession hit, and most companies were scaling back and not hiring new people. She then realized that her situation was desperate. She lost her apartment and started living out of her car.

One day on the beach several friendly girls took an interest in her situation. They belonged to a commune that welcomed people like herself and let them stay until they were able to get on their feet again. Considering these girls an answer to prayer, she moved onto their large estate, studied meditation with the group leader, and grew organic vegetables for the commune's food supply. Her situation looked great. She was getting thinner and eating more healthful foods, and she was getting in touch with herself and her body through transcendental meditation. It was fun working together with so many other devotees. They cleaned the toilets, worked in the gardens, and sold the commune goods to the local community.

One day, while cleaning the kitchen, she noticed several large steaks in the freezer. When she asked one of the leaders what they were doing there, she was told, "They are for the guru's use in sacrifice." "Sacrifice, what kind of sacrifice?" she asked. "The sacrifice to the spirits when the steak is burned," he replied, "before he puts on the A1 Sauce and eats it!" She then realized the game that was going on. The devotees ate vegetables while their guru got to "sacrifice" steaks. The whole picture then began to fit together. He was running a little business in the guise of meditation and a cult. His workers received no pay but did all the work, including all the housework and upkeep for the mansion. Worse, she found out that she was not really free to leave. Doors were locked from the outside every night, and "greeters" were always standing at the doors.

One night she took a good look at herself in the mirror and realized what she had become: not an actress or a wealthy man's wife but a household servant...no, it was worse...she was a slave! Suddenly, a flash of insight occurred. She remembered her father. She thought, *Here I am eating these crummy vegetables and soups, while my brothers and sisters are back in Jersey enjoying a lovely, well-cooked Italian meal. I will sneak out of this place and go home.* She tied some sheets together and slid out her window into the yard. Over the wall she went and, finding the first car headed east, she hitchhiked all the way back to Jersey. As she walked up the steps to her home, her father was standing at the door and ran to her, embracing her with tears in his eyes. She said, "Daddy, I've made such a mess out of my life, please just let me live here for a while, and I'll work for you and repay all the money that I lost. I am no longer worthy of anything." Her father called to the rest of the family, "Warm up the leftovers and break out a bottle of champagne. Tonight we celebrate because my daughter who left has come home!"[29]

Obviously, the story is more than just an illustration. It is a paraphrase of the story Jesus told a group of religious leaders who were very confused about how they thought God should behave. Jesus' reply to them was the story of the prodigal son (see Luke 15:11–32), which showed that no matter where we are or what has happened to us, this is what our God is like: compassionate, accepting, understanding, and present! John White has observed,

Although repentance may indeed be painful, it does not come about as a response to severity. Stern accusation and recrimination may exacerbate our feelings of guilt and shame but they never give rise to true repentance. . . . The relief of knowing we might be loved and accepted is what brings true change.[30]

In a way, trauma makes us all prodigals. No matter how loving our God may be, we view Him as our enemy and have to flee from His presence for a while. We have to go it alone in our pain. But there also comes a time when we must come to our senses and realize that healing begins back in His presence. Presence is what brings healing. Only a person can be present. God is a Person, the ultimate Person who provides the presence we need to begin the healing process. What is interesting to me is the quotation from Jesus that opened this chapter (see Matt. 5:4). Jesus said that the cure for those who mourn is comfort. Comfort during grieving comes only from a person, either in a friend who becomes our mourning partner or in God, whose supernatural presence is the comfort we need when we return home. God provides His presence for those made in His image. But healing only begins here. Healing also involves forgiveness.

Healing Means Receiving and Extending Forgiveness

As noted earlier in this chapter, some who work in the field of inner healing ignore the moral dimensions of trauma. Rape victims, Holocaust victims, hostages, those who have lost jobs, abused spouses and children—all these would seem to have a right to their feelings without being concerned about the morality of those feelings. They have every right to their feelings. But the important question is how harmful the feelings of hate, anger, resentment, and bitterness are to their personal health and relationships. Let's face it: we don't win friends and influence people with these emotions. They can drive even the people who love us away. So in the absence of forgiveness there are not many options. Each of the above emotional reactions is justifiable in its origin but not necessarily healthy over the long term. Even though tragedies are thrust upon individuals with terrific force, the reactions over time can produce even more difficulties. When individuals have been traumatized by other people, it would seem that the moral element must be dealt with. We have observed that we humans are moral beings. It's just not smart to ignore this principle. If we are moral beings, then issues of fairness and justice stand at the heart of our healing. John White articulated a well-balanced caution:

> Unless the moral aspects of the problem—which include the response of the person doing the remembering—are faced, the experience is unlikely to lead to permanent change. . . . You can pursue the healing of memories in vain if this principle is ignored.[31]

To talk of fairness and justice is to speak of our desire for punishment. When I have been wronged, I want my "pound of flesh," my ounce of retribution, my opportunity to see the one who hurt me pay for his wrong. Whether or not we realize it, the trauma always raises the issue of morality and punishment. And it works both ways. When I have done evil to another person, something within me knows that I deserve punishment. In the absence of punishment I punish myself to atone for my sins.

The kind of forgiveness I am talking about is not some kindhearted, sugar-daddy kind of mercy, the kind that says, "That's OK, no problem" but that does not cost anyone anything. True forgiveness costs! It's an amazing principle. To declare their commitment as blood brothers, Indians bond through shedding blood. In primitive societies everything from business deals to marriages were closed with either an animal's giving up its life or a person's giving up something as a pledge. Forming new relationships and restoring old relationships always had significant costs attached to them. The same is true of God's forgiveness of us. We find our forgiveness in the innocent blood of Jesus the Messiah, who died in our place as our substitute. In a sense, God took the initiative to bond with the world through the death of His own son. That's a costly forgiveness. But you may ask, "Why is this important for the one who has been victimized by events beyond his or her control?" Good question. Lewis Smedes has an excellent reply:

> Forgiving is love's revolution against life's unfairness. When we forgive, we ignore the normal law that straps us to the natural law of getting even and, by the alchemy of love, we release ourselves from our own pasts. We fly over a dues-paying morality in order to create a new future out of the past's unfairness. We free ourselves from the wrong that is locked into our private histories, we unshackle our spirits from malice; and maybe, if we are lucky, we also restore a relationship that would otherwise be lost forever.[32]

Did you hear his language? True forgiveness is a release, a freeing from what holds us in bondage. The biblical words translated as "forgiveness" reflect this idea of release.[33] God can forgive us and release us from our sins because of Jesus' death on the cross. It was there on the cross that the penalty for our crimes was paid, whereby we stand released from moral debt toward God. This pardon, then, becomes the ground on which we can forgive and release others from the harm they have done to us. Leanne Payne has noted:

Although not all our relationships with other people can be healed in this life, we can forgive and release everyone who is unable to love or accept us, or unable to relate to us in a manner pleasing to God. We can by the Grace of God, forgive those who have so deeply wounded us. As we forgive them, we find that not only do our own wounds heal, but our experience becomes the source of healing knowledge and power for others.[34]

Healing is facilitated faster and easier when the guilty party asks for forgiveness and we respond accordingly or when we have the opportunity to confront our abuser, and he responds by recognizing his wrong. This is the principle Jesus taught: "If your brother sins against you, rebuke him; and if he repents, forgive him" (Luke 17:3). When this is not possible, we have to release the person from moral wrong against us. How can this be done? I agree with Smedes that forgiveness, in the final analysis, is a miracle. But he also noted the realistic human struggle with forgiveness. This struggle makes forgiveness a slow process, a process that is helped by our trying to understand the one who hurt us; confusion will be common, with some anger being left over, but it takes place little by little, involves great emotional risk, and begins with the fundamental feeling of being forgiven ourselves.[35]

This moral aspect of forgiveness is what the patriarch Job struggled with. He knew and pleaded his own innocence before his friends and God. However, his friends condemned him for being self-righteous. In this act Job's friends had wronged him. Both God and his other friend, Elihu, confronted these "comforters" with their wrong (Job 32:3). As an appropriate act of penance they are told to sacrifice seven bulls and seven rams in front of Job (Job 42:8), a costly penance even in modern agricultural terms. But what about Job's inner healing? The text says that Job's fortunes were not restored *until* he prayed for his friends, the ones who hurt him (Job 42:10). This is probably one of the greatest acts that both demonstrates and initiates the process of forgiveness. Whether it is praying for the Vietnamese, or praying for the unknown rapist, or praying for those who released the hostages in Lebanon, when we begin to pray for those who have hurt us, healing can begin to take place in our hearts.

God's forgiveness is also the basis for self-forgiveness. For the traumas created by personal moral failure (like sexual sins, theft, and killing), the message is the same. Jesus has already been tried and convicted for the failure. He was punished for this crime; therefore, I need both to accept the forgiveness from God and to apply it to myself. If I don't forgive myself, I am in fact saying that God's punishment of Jesus was not enough for me. I have to add punishment to it. My refusal either to forgive others or to forgive myself is ultimately a rejection of God and what He has done for me!

One other element is important to consider at this point. While working on this chapter, I reached this particular point and realized I needed to say something about whether it is ever appropriate to say that we forgive God for what He has allowed to happen to us. I threw out the concept to my faculty colleagues, who in turn discussed the pros and cons of such a statement. The problem in traditional theological terms is in ascribing error or wrong to God. If we need to forgive God, it implies that God wronged us! But I argue that the problem is not on God's end of the stick. I believe that God is truly benevolent, but I cannot see His purposes. What happens to me is, from my perception, God's wronging me with tragic events that could have been avoided. In human relationships one can do harm to others when all the motives are good and proper. A mother can do her best to love and nurture her children, but often they view this love as violence, manipulation, or smothering. Harm does not necessarily lie in the intent of the subject but in the perception of the receiver. Could it be the same in our relationships with God? If forgiveness from both the biblical and psychological definitions means to release one from wrongs committed, is there a time when we need to release God from even our perception that He has wronged us? Does this hurt His feelings? Smedes observed, "Would it bother God too much if we found our peace by forgiving him for wrongs we suffer? What if we found a way to forgive him without blaming him? A special sort of forgiving for a special sort of relationship. Would he mind?"[36] The point of this discussion is that it may be therapeutically valuable for the traumatized individual mentally to release God from the perceived wrong. This may be an important step in facilitating the recovery process and changing the way of thinking about God. Later, when the benevolent purposes of God can be seen, the experience can be brought more in line with the thinking. Smedes concluded, "I think we may need to forgive God after all. Now and then, but not often. Not for his sake. For ours! So let us talk of healing ourselves as we forgive God."[37]

As important as forgiveness is to the healing process, there is another aspect to the healing of memories.

Healing Takes a Gracious Relationship

In the physical realm not all chronic pain is healed. Many individuals must learn to live with pain. I believe this is also the case with psychic pain. Some memories are severe, emotionally deep, and a part of who we have become.

The greatest leader in the early church was one who had serious chronic pain. It wouldn't go away, even though he asked God to do an inner healing. After much struggle (and probably the best medical advice, since the physician Luke was always with him) and pain, God blasted him with a new insight: "My grace is sufficient for you, for My strength is made perfect in weakness" (2 Cor. 12:9). This was a good news/bad news report. The bad news was simply "Paul, I am not going to heal you." The good news was "But you can live with your pain, and, in fact, you will be stronger because of it." That's the new frame God put around the picture of Paul's pain. The nonhealing answer God gave was that of a gracious relationship.

Grace is not a commodity that can be purchased or packaged. Some throughout church history have tried to barter and market it as if it were. But these attempts have also perverted the true nature of what grace is all about. Grace is not something God gives to us in the abstract or the material. Grace is an attribute of a person. When attached to God, it says that He is a gracious person. He then deals with us in accordance with who He really is. Since He is a gracious Person, He deals with us graciously. My own definition for what *grace* means is "the power of celebrative joy and favor."[38] God's unconditional joy and favor toward us are the sources of our well-being, even in the midst of pain and suffering. The support and comfort that come from knowing that one Person will never change in His regard toward me become my sufficiency to live daily even with psychic pain. Grace means that God likes me even in my pain, suffering, and running away from Him. He understands my pain, feels my pain, but also knows that I will learn some things through it that I could not learn any other way. There is a well-being that is derived not from my own well-being but from God's, as activated through Jesus. Grace means that I can live with psychic pain. Grace is the rehabilitative power that allows me to keep hoping and keep on going, even when my pain says otherwise. As I am writing this chapter, the remaining American hostages have been released from their Lebanese captors. They have told stories of extreme isolation, torture, and deprivation. How did they survive? A *Time* article underscored their means of coping with extreme psychic pain:

What pulled the men through such moments of hopelessness? For Sutherland it was thoughts of his wife, three daughters, and a grandson he had never seen. For Anderson it was a Bible and a photograph of his daughter Sulome, now six, whom he met for the first time last week. Men with strong religious affiliations relied heavily on their spiritual muscles. Three bare wires hanging from the ceiling evoked for Rev. Benjamin Weir the fingers of the painting on the ceiling of the Sistine Chapel. "That became to me a representation of the sustaining, purposeful hand of God," he recalls. Others discovered a faith they never knew they had. "Before, I didn't believe in God and now I do," Frenchman Roger Auque told the British press after his 319 days in captivity.[39]

What was this? Some unrealistic, demented hope that isolation from all human contact breeds? Or was it a very real, supernatural power that daily gave these men a reason to go on? The encouragement received from Bibles, from even cords dangling from the ceiling, it would seem that God used as sources of grace. Instead of succumbing, giving up, or giving in, they continued with enough hope to stay alive. This is the power of grace, which God promises to those who fully realize they will never rid themselves of their pain.

Besides, I'm not sure that I want all my pain or the pain of others to be healed. It is the well-articulated pain of others that becomes the source of encouragement and hope to other sufferers. If the pain were healed, where would the co-sharers of suffering be? Personally, I'm glad that people like Mary Beyers Garrison have not been healed of pain. Her poetry and the emotional logging of others' experiences can touch the hurting human spirit in ways that only one who is still in pain can communicate. She recorded:

> They didn't say much in recovery, especially the head
> wounded,
> Airway pulled, vital signs stable, heads raised,
> Ready to roll over to ward 5.
> Some called it the vegetable patch.
> Not forty-five minutes out of surgery, head big with bandages
> One side of his body paralyzed like an old man
> This one was wide awake and flirting.
> "Hey, you're cute," he said.
> Surprised and flattered, I grinned wide
> and wished I really was cute.
> Twenty years later his next words still turn me cold.
> "I was a steeplejack."

> Mary Beyers Garrison
> U.S. Army Nurse Corps
> Long Binh, Vietnam[40]

Poetry like hers becomes an agent of grace to those who read it. Merely reading about the hurts of others brings this sense of joyous favor about painful experiences. I noticed this on my first trip to the "wall." During a military chaplains' conference we spent one afternoon milling around the monuments in Washington, D.C. I was with a chaplain who had served in Vietnam not as a chaplain but as a grunt. He told me he had known many in his unit who had been "blown away" in Vietnam. When we got to the Vietnam Memorial, it became a sacred moment. As a matter of fact, I always feel a sense of the sacred at this monument unlike at any others in D.C. I watched my friend. After looking up the names of his buddies and finding them on the wall, he paused for several minutes in front of the names. I noticed tears in his eyes as he moved from name to name. Finally, he turned around and looked at me and broke into a smile. His combination of tears and a smile threw me. It seemed inappropriate, out of place here at the "American wailing wall." Still smiling, he said, "I remember some great times with those guys. I really miss them." There it was. A joyous favor breaking out of nowhere into this veteran's heart and culminating in a smile. I am convinced that this expression emerged not from within but from without. In times of our deepest sorrow God can break through with hope, a joyous memory, a picture of our family, that puts a smile on our face even in the midst of pain.

The concept of gracious relationships also spills over into the area of support groups. In my opinion, what has happened in our culture is that support groups have largely taken over the role of the confessional in the Catholic tradition and the open sharing of problems in the protestant tradition. For whatever reasons, the recovery movement, beginning with Alcoholics Anonymous, has created a climate that is needed for healing to take place. Support groups have been successful because they create a climate in which any emotion or statement can be aired without critical evaluation. What is created is an atmosphere of gracious acceptance. What the Catholic church and biblical Christianity have known for centuries is now being used by almost all therapists in their support groups (see James 5:14–16; 1 John 1:9). Healing takes place when we hear others reveal their hurts, sins, and struggles and when we reveal our own in a context of acceptance and affirmation. Whether a person is recovering from abuse, or divorce, or a natural disaster, or war, healing takes place in community. It is hard to heal alone. Healing requires the gracious relationships of other brother and sister survivors. Perhaps that's another reason why Jesus said, "Where two or three are gathered together in My name, I am there in the midst of them" (Matt. 18:20). A mysterious, supernatural uplifting can take place when individuals center themselves on the common agreement to support one another; confess their failures, fears, and feelings to one another; and see the healing that comes only from Jesus take place. But still another aspect of healing is important.

Memorializing Our Pain

It was mentioned earlier the role the Vietnam Memorial has played in helping veterans commemorate their experience and, more importantly, in helping facilitate their grief and loss. If you have not been to the wall in D.C., it is an experience worth the time. Even if you do not know anyone in the war, go just to watch the sacred moments of others.

It is a memorial to pain. Hardened veterans who have not given Vietnam much thought break down and weep at the wall. Adult children who never knew their dads who got killed in Vietnam weep. Wives, grandparents, friends, fraternity brothers, relatives all come, write notes, place flowers, inscribe names on pieces of tracing paper, all in tribute not only to the one who died but also to their own grief, even twenty years later. One of the things researchers have learned in this field is the important role of memorials in starting the grief process and in facilitating continued healing.

Our weekend at the Dallas-Fort Worth Hilton was so wild that the last thing I thought about was planning a worship service on Sunday. The plane crashed on Friday afternoon, and Saturday was a long day, as families and relatives moved into the hotel and we issued death notifications. However, by Saturday evening friends and family members alike began asking the priest and me whether we would have services in the hotel the next morning. Hurriedly, at about eleven o'clock on Saturday night we made plans for both Catholic and general protestant services the next morning. We advertised the services on the hotel's television channel. Our Catholic service was scheduled first, with the protestant following immediately. Both were kept short. At times like these the familiar is important. For protestants we sang a familiar hymn, I read Psalm 23, and then I gave a brief homily on the death of Lazarus and described how his sisters, Mary and Martha, were so angry with Jesus. I used the text to elicit from those gathered the feelings of loss, anger at God (Jesus), and the blaming that is common in disaster reactions. It was the hardest service I have ever done. At the end many, including protestants, Catholics, and others, were gathered outside the door wanting to come in, but they had arrived late, having just seen the announcement on television. They were angry —at me, at the hotel for not advertising the services better, and because we had shut the doors. I was surprised by the anger and the commitment to worship even in a time of severe stress and grief. It was one of those times when I was slow to get the point. These grievers wanted to give expression to their loss in a ceremonial way.

Quickly, the priest, the rabbi, and I put together a joint ecumenical memorial service for that evening. We had this one widely advertised by means of television and fliers circulated throughout the hotel. That evening the ballroom was packed with families, friends, and hotel and Delta Airlines personnel. We had several Scripture readings, prayers, and meditations. Then, at our priest's request, Father Brown opened the service to the congregants. He encouraged them to tell God how they felt. I personally was skeptical. But one by one individuals began to pour out their grief, anger, and dismay to God. I saw before my eyes the therapeutic effect. At the end of the service families stood up and for the first time recognized that others were grieving as well. Up to this time, throughout the hotel, in the restaurant or just walking around, families would group together and eat, walk, or grieve alone. I considered this a breakthrough. Spontaneously, everyone stood up and began embracing other families. The memorial service had solidified the families. They then realized that they were a part of a shared grief, that others needed their touch and understanding, an understanding that only those who had lost loved ones could provide. This service was one of the most wonderful experiences of my life. I wish I had a videotape of the experience. This memorializing of grief brought a sense of healing and gave permission to grieve in new ways. That's what memorials do.

For some time therapists have talked about anniversary grief. This is a recognized difficult time for grieving family members and friends. Therefore, this is an excellent time to use the anniversary to help continue the healing process, as well as to give vent and structure to the anniversary grief reactions.[41] In natural disasters or air crashes it is good to have memorial services for those who were lost and for the survivors to continue working through their grief reactions. One therapist has written:

> Rituals are a part of every social group. They are found in a surprising variety of forms and are practiced in some manner by all societies. Rituals can provide powerful therapeutic experiences that symbolize transition, healing, and continuity. Consequently, they can address and catalyze many aspects of the grief process. Like funerals, they can initiate the process of grief. However, they are not magic. Their power comes from the faith that the individual has in their ability to provide meaning.[42]

I agree with this statement but would add that I believe there is more healing power to this than the faith of the individual. I believe God can *really* bring His healing presence into these services to work at a much deeper level than what the mere faith of the individual brings. I have seen it and heard about it in the lives of POWs, hostages, and trauma victims of all kinds.

For a couple who lost a child in their own backyard swimming pool I suggested having a memorial service one year later both to remember their lost child and to provide a "reframing" experience for the pool, which had not been used after the drowning. In this area I believe clergy and therapists can work hand in hand to deal better with many normal grief reactions that are associated with anniversaries. We need to take our pain and make memorials out of them.

Speaking of memorials, I wish to end this chapter by putting on my clergy cap. Again, in this area I am amazed that the secular literature and research suggest something profoundly theological in nature. The writer quoted above has stated that the role of rituals is to "allow the griever to express his inner feelings and expiate his feelings of guilt." She went on to point out that rituals:

> legitimize emotional ventilation, channel feelings of grief, assist in the mourning of unresolved grief, provide a structure focusing on the grief, while also allowing for participation by others as a social group and consequently creating a celebration from the normal grief reactions.[43]

Unknowingly, what the writer has described is the tradition known in the Christian church as holy Communion or the Lord's Table.

Unfortunately, in many Christian traditions this sacred element has lost much of its original meaning. Traditionally, the ceremony recognizes the brokenness and death of our Savior, Jesus Christ, on behalf of those who accept Him as their Redeemer and King. The table[44] is, then, a place of forgiveness and acceptance centered both on the receiver's acknowledged brokenness and sinfulness and on the brokenness and sinlessness of Christ. It provides either the symbolic or actual divine human connection in the pain of Christ. It is a place where we bring our brokenness and pain and connect it with the brokenness and pain of Christ. This unity, which is created in the shared fellowship with the sufferings of Christ, is what the meaning of the church is all about. One Vietnam veteran told me that the only time he really felt forgiven for his crimes in Vietnam was when he took holy Communion. It provided a focus that he needed. As he went forward to receive the elements and as he took the elements into himself, he could visualize Jesus bringing healing to his soul. Perhaps, whether we see this ritual as sacrament or ordinance, this is the memorialization God has given to the church and the world in which all our pain and traumas can be visualized and sanctified, forgiveness can be experienced, and inner healing can take place.

Linn and Linn reveal the attitude in which the receiver should come in order to find healing in this ritual:

> This is the time to give Jesus all my anger and pray, "Lord have mercy" toward me and all who have hurt me. When I can bring to the opening penitential rite a memory of someone who has hurt me and tell the Lord how I feel, then reconciliation and healing can begin.... Eucharistic healing occurs when we give Christ our hardened, unforgiving hearts and receive His heart of flesh opened on Calvary. There He released to us His forgiving Spirit as promised, "A new heart I will give you and a new Spirit I will put within you; and I will take out of your flesh the heart of stone and give you a heart of flesh" (Ezek. 36:26). Memories are healed when hearts are exchanged on Calvary.[45]

It is in this Eucharistic memorial that our screams meet the scream of God in the symbolic blood of His own Son.

In conclusion, it would seem that many factors are involved in healing the screams of the traumatized. Scurfield has noted five key principles for the treatment of stress disorders:

1. The establishment of a therapeutic trust relationship.
2. Education about the stress-recovery process.
3. Working with the traumatized to learn how to reduce or live with the stress.
4. Helping the traumatized reexperience and recollect the trauma in the here and now.
5. Final integration of the trauma into the notions of who the survivor was before and after the experience. In this sense, clarification, atonement, and penance may be crucial for dealing with guilt.[46]

This researcher is saying that in order to facilitate our own healing, we need someone in our lives with whom we can trust our feelings; we need some basic information about what is to be expected and what is normal for what we have been through; we need to learn some basic techniques so that we know what to do when the flooding of memories takes place or when the panic attacks hit; we need someone to help us relive all the details of our trauma and to articulate not only the facts but also the feelings at that time and now; finally, we ultimately need to be able to "reframe" the trauma, to bring it back into our new frame of reality. This may take serious moral clarification, forgiveness, and other steps that will free us from the guilt and psychic pain we bear. Throughout these processes using our faith in God and other spiritual resources is critical to healing. Also, finding a group of people with whom we can do all of these together is probably one of the most important principles. If there is any consensus regarding treatment, it is that a multimethod approach is best.[47] No one method is ideal or will work for everyone.

One question, however, awaits from this discussion. The question is basic. Can we do anything to prepare for traumas so that they do not have such a terrible impact on us?

If it is possible, as much as depends on you, live peaceably with all men.

Romans 12:18

CONCLUSION

Can We Prepare for Traumatic Events?

"**C**an we prepare for traumatic events?" I don't know how many times I have heard the question. But each time I do, I make a quiet inner vow to myself. During the aftermath of the Delta crash the question was prefaced by many other statements. They were poignant remarks, said with much deeply felt regret and remorse. The statements had several variations on a theme, but they all came out the same way. Throughout the week after the crash, individuals would say to me, "I wish I could have said...; I wish I had known...; I wish I had done.... Variations on the same theme. The theme? The theme of regret! What people wish they could have done, said, or resolved before the crash. A mother said, "I wish I could have told my daughter how proud I was of her." A father lamented that he should have told his son he loved him. A divorced man said, "I wish I could have told Mary that being married to her wasn't as bad as I made her think it was. I really did love her." Hearing these statements all day and night affects one very deeply. They affected me. When I finally went home, I vowed to myself that I would never take another trip without telling my wife and kids how much I love them.

I learned from my experiences in that extended house of mourning at the Dallas-Fort Worth Hilton that most people are not prepared for trauma. But they could be. Who would even think about preparing for the unlikely and the worst-case scenario? Oh, we may put smoke alarms in our homes and plan the fire and emergency escapes, but we really don't think through the human elements. Yet it is the human-relationship issues that make surviving traumas so difficult, especially when regret is involved. So what can be done to prepare for the possible traumas that may come our way?

For some time researchers have studied a concept called heartiness. Heartiness is referred to as a "dispositional style," mixed with a particular kind of social support, which makes traumatic events less damaging for the one experiencing them.[1] Horowitz was one of the first to articulate the extent to which people vary significantly in their responses to traumatic stress. From studying these varying response factors, one can gain insights into how people might better prepare themselves not only for extreme traumas but also for minor ones. It is now believed that the pivotal factors that make up this hearty personality include the manners or ways by which people approach their lives and how they interpret their experiences. These hearty personalities carry with them to the trauma a sense of commitment that gives them a certain meaning and purpose to their lives and the world. They also carry with them a sense of autonomy that gives them an important perception of influence or control over their environment, no matter what happens. Lastly, these hearty ones bring to the trauma a zest for life that allows them to see the changed circumstances as opportunities for growth rather than threats to their security.[2] In some Israeli studies, active coping skills were the best and most striking factors predicting which combat soldiers did not develop high rates of posttraumatic-stress disorders.[3] What all this means in lay terms is that the average person can do some things to prepare for life traumas.

The Quality of Our Existing Relationships

It is hoped that in the quotations throughout the book the idea of a social network has been noticed frequently. The person who survives trauma the best is the one who has preexisting quality relationships in his life. Notice the POWs, the hostages, and other victims. They thank God for their families predominantly. This is the primary social network that gives our life meaning and sustains us through difficult times. It would make sense, then, that the best way to prepare for traumas is to make sure these primary relationships are what they ought to be. We should seek to keep short accounts on the conflict ledger of our relationships. We need to ask ourselves, *Where I am in my relationships with my children, with my parents, with my spouse, and with my close friends?* This is my social network, which becomes a lifeline when trauma hits. When I fly, before I get on the airplane, I sometimes wonder if I need to make some phone calls before the plane takes off. I may realize that I didn't leave home the way I should have and that I left some important relationships dangling. How many times do we not give the basic maintenance to our closest relationships and therefore have to work through many regrets when traumas hit? Working through the unresolved guilt and leftover emotional baggage makes for an even more difficult adjustment when crisis hits. In actuality this becomes a second trauma.

I would also put in this category of important relationships our relationship with God. As seen throughout this book, many of the issues inherent in the field of trauma studies have serious theological and spiritual significance. Also, the reader should have noted on the subject of heartiness that having meaning also plays a very important role as a predisposition factor. The person who has a genuine, vibrant, and realistic faith has a frame that can provide the needed meaning when no other meaning is found. Our faith can often make sense of the absurd. In this area there exists a certain "soul heartiness" that makes one more prepared for the traumas of life than the person without a genuine faith. In prosperous and good times this element of survivorship is sometimes laughed at. But when hostages are released or earthquake victims are interviewed, they usually attribute their well-being to their faith in God. Their testimonies are often laughed at off camera by the press, but the experiences of victims and the growing social research confirm that this tough faith provides an element of meaning to the person. It should not be in any way minimized as irrelevant or counterproductive to the recovery process. Each of us should occasionally take a spiritual inventory.

In this light we need to ask ourselves whether our relationship with God is what it ought to be. Many walk around daily with good intentions, making the New Year's resolution type of commitments to God and the church. However, rarely do they follow through on these commitments. There are always those who find God in the foxholes, but the story of how they live when they return home is usually not told. It is better to go to the foxhole with a relationship with God intact than to go with a strained or non-existent one.

Hopeful Tenacity

It is very difficult to document or describe this subject, but I believe that one of the best ways to prepare for potential traumas is to develop the habit of hopeful tenacity. I am not quite sure what it is, but I have seen it. I have seen it in victims of the worst sort. Somehow they have developed or have been blessed from above with a hopeful tenacity not only to "hang in there" in the midst of severe psychic and physical pain but also to be hopeful. I have seen it in cancer patients with terminal illness, in HIV-positive Christians, in parents who have lost children, in veterans living with war trauma, and in Dennis, a very special friend. Dennis has had multiple sclerosis for over twenty years. He is in a wheelchair, has very little control over his body, and has progressively deteriorated over the course of twenty years. However, in spirit he is a giant. He has not only MS but also the incurable disease of a hopeful spirit despite all odds.

Dennis lived with us for about six months. Our house was not the best for his wheelchair and physical well-being. Our dining room was converted into his bedroom so that he could be near a bathroom on our first floor. However, our small bathroom was only a half bath, so we had to carry Dennis to the second floor to bathe him. For this period in our lives Dennis became a member of the family. Our family took care of him physically, but Dennis enriched our lives spiritually and emotionally. I don't ever remember his complaining, even when he was completely fevered and immobilized with the flu. Once he spent the early-morning hours lying on the floor after falling out of bed. He didn't want to wake up the rest of us! Instead of complaining, Dennis has always remained hopeful, with a tenacity that defies all human reason. He writes poetry, books, and music. For years he has taught ghetto kids how to read and has given them a vision for improving their lives. Five years ago he married a special woman, and they are very happy. As I write this conclusion, we have just received Dennis's standard Christmas poem, updating us on all the family events of the past year. It portrays his usual hopeful spirit, a spirit of love, thankfulness, and optimism. What drives Dennis is his faith in Jesus Christ. This is no pie-in-the-sky faith; it is faith manifested in the trenches of life. It is a faith that gives him a hopeful tenacity about life.

It is this same hopeful tenacity that led one veteran into a ministry of counseling other veterans. One middle-aged veteran had been wrestling with the demons of Vietnam for years. Finally, in desperation he was given a counselor's name. When the man walked into the counselor's office, he noticed a man in a wheelchair with no legs and only one arm. The startled, intact veteran vocalized his first impressions: "My God, I can't talk to you." The counselor returned, "I can understand that. You can very easily see the pain I bear every day, but I can't see your pain. Maybe you would like to talk about it." That was the door to the fellow veteran's bruised and battered soul. He began pouring out his pain to the tenacious counselor who held out hope to his fellow veteran.[4]

These examples illustrate that the best preparation for trauma is cultivating a hopeful spirit in normal times. Having a hopeful spirit some may see as a special gift or a function of a special personality type. But a hopeful attitude toward life is available to all human beings. At some point we must realize that how we view our lives, including the traumas that have happened to us, is our choice. It is not determined by circumstances, breaks, traumas, or the lack of these. Life may take us down many roads that are bumpy or hazardous, but even along these roads may lie some beautiful scenery. Even Auschwitz survivors confessed seeing an early-morning sunrise through the cracks in their prison walls and thinking how beautiful the morning was. The scene provided a new ray of hope in the midst of death and decay. Somehow many of these survivors had enough hope within them to continue. We can practice this attitude daily, and in so doing, prepare ourselves for potential traumas that may await us.

A Large Picture Frame

Much has been said in this book about framing and the need for reframing. The frame holds our assumptions about life. Chapter 1 explained how these assumptions are shattered by trauma. What was not said is that many of our assumptions are not quite on target. Some assumptions about life are better than others when it comes to surviving and preparing for traumas. We live in such a relativistic age that it seems out of place to say that any belief might be wrong. But in the field of trauma some beliefs are better than others. What we need to prepare better for traumatic events is a very large frame. A large frame is one in which true reality can be placed. It is a frame that is true to reality. This means that the frame must allow for the genuine possibility that something bad, evil, or traumatic could happen. I don't believe this is being pessimistic or paranoid. In fact, it would seem that this perspective is better suited to the potential and actual realities we face every day. Then if something of an evil nature happens to us, it does not shatter our total belief system to the same extent as if we held to the assumption of invulnerability.

Likewise, our assumptions should allow for irrationality in life, as opposed to assuming that everything should make sense in this life. The frame of irrationality does not say that the entire world is an irrational place, but it does say that we can't figure everything out. Things happen that in and of themselves may never give a satisfactory answer. This is where our faith and hope may come to play an important role, providing a certain meaning where there is none. The larger frame also gives us an understanding that we should not expect the world to deal with us in all fairness and justice. We should certainly work for such things and never be unjust or act unjustly because the world may not always be fair. But to be adequately prepared for potential traumas, we must give up the expectation that everything in life be fair. We are moral beings, and we have an acute, God-given sense of justice; but this is not a perfect world. We face a fallen, evil world either in ourselves or in others almost every day. Injustice happens, and when it happens to me, it surprises me. We need to widen the frame and allow our assumptions about life to have more of a fallen reality in them.

Lastly, to prepare for traumas, it is important to recognize where my identity really exists. It rides on my relationships and how well my life is going. I am very much entangled with and networked into the lives of other people. I am a husband, a son, a father, a brother, a professor, a clergyman, a U.S. Air Force officer, a citizen, a skier, and a tennis player. Take any of these away from me, and I suffer a sense of loss. No, I don't suffer a sense of loss; I suffer loss! I have lost an important part of who I am. My identity rides on my relationships. Maybe, to prepare better for traumas that might come into my life, I need to rethink who I am. Am I secure within myself, apart from all the roles I play and the responsibilities I fulfill? Where do I find my well-being? How do I see myself apart from the important people in my life?

I am certainly not suggesting that the well-prepared person is the rugged individualist who has no relationships with other people. No, that person has his own problems. But what I am talking about is having *too* much of my identity riding on either the roles I play or the people in my life. We can have too much of our own identity enmeshed with our kids, our spouses, or our jobs. Consequently, when these are lost or not going well, we become traumatized.

For those who find valuable meaning in their relationship with Christ, the identity of being a Christian plays an equally important role. We might ask how much of our identity is found in this unconditional, personal relationship. These are helpful questions to ask ourselves in preparation for what might happen to us. The answers are even more important!

Vocational Satisfaction

Frankly, I have been very surprised by how many vocational-dissatisfaction issues have become intertwined with the recovery issues of trauma. In doing follow-up with those I worked closely with in the Delta crash, I found very few still employed by Delta. In my work with military personnel I found the same disillusionment with careers following severe crises. In private counseling I have seen that it is common for individuals to change careers after major traumatic events in their lives. As I understand what happens in trauma, I have come to the following conclusion. Trauma brings to the surface all the dissatisfaction in our lives. Since one of our major identity roles is found in our jobs and careers, if this area is producing a generous amount of satisfaction, then work can become a place of therapy for the traumatized. If, on the other hand, it is a place of dissatisfaction, then the dissatisfaction turns to total disillusionment. In response, the individual, often within the year of the tragedy, leaves the job or career.

What this says to most of us in the pretrauma stage is that we can prepare for traumas by being in the kind of employment we enjoy. I don't think all aspects of our work should be pleasing, but at least we should have a reasonable amount of satisfaction with the labor of our hands. It seems to make good sense to ask ourselves, *Am I doing with my life what I really want to do?* If the answer is no, it might say that I am in a precarious position for dealing with trauma effectively. I still remember the night I was ordained to the ministry. After the formal service a reception was held in my honor. A man in late middle age said to me, "It is so nice to see young men going into the ministry. I was called to the ministry when I was in my twenties, but I never went." Almost without thinking, I replied, "What makes you think God calls only once?" Wouldn't it be better to spend the last ten years of one's life where one ought to be than to spend forty or fifty in dissatisfaction? Not only is this common sense, but it also could be a unique buffer against the wiles of traumatic stressors when they hit with full vengeance.

Living on Both Sides of the Street

What this book has tried to do is to acquaint the reader with this increasingly more common human reaction to trauma called posttraumatic-stress disorder. We are a traumatized society. Whether the trauma is perceived as great or small by others is irrelevant when we are on the receiving end. Traumatic events, whether they involve being in an auto accident, being told one is HIV-positive, being raped, or recovering from the impact of Vietnam or Desert Storm, live on within us. They show up wherever we go. We carry something that is toxic. It is a disease with harmful effects on us and on those who have to live with us. Therefore, it needs to be understood; appreciated for its unique elements; and, hopefully, accepted as a normal reaction to abnormal events. The traumatized person may have some peculiar quirks, but so would anyone else who had gone through the same tragic circumstances. The good news is that the worst events are survivable. Only when the traumatized isolate themselves and begin to think that no one understands them is surviving difficult. But when the pain, fears, and inner rage are shared with others who have suffered similar fates, the victim can begin to see that the responses are normal. With time, understanding, acceptance, and the spiritual resources outlined in this book, trauma can be survived, and the person can move on with hope.

However, when the traumatized move on, they are never the same. They view life differently because of their traumatic experiences. They have screamed, and the scream leaves them different...for the rest of life. A radiant but teary-eyed Sergeant Bobbie Trotter paused momentarily during our reservist weekend to read me her poem reflecting this "returning-home" memory. Some twenty years after the war this "Donut Dollie" wrote:

I Know You've Waited

I know you've waited
A long, hard time for me
And yes, I am coming home.
But in all fairness,
I am not the same person you loved then.
We'll need time.[6]

The traumatized are normal for what they have been through, but they need time and understanding. The street of life has two sides to it. Both sides are normal for what they represent. One side reflects all the good and pleasurable things of life. This is where most of us would like to build our houses, move in, and stay for the rest of our lives. However, traumatic events move us to another side of life, which immobilizes and paralyzes us for a time. This is just as normal. As one looks at those on the other side of life, it is difficult to understand how they can carry on or go through such things. Misunderstanding is common. However, life involves both the good and the bad, the pleasurable and the ignoble. The key to life is learning to live on both sides of the street simultaneously, neither ignoring the possibilities and realities of evil nor enjoying the best our world has to offer.

Ann Rosenburg is a survivor who has lived on both sides of the street. She graphically portrays what life was like on "the other side of the street," the side of pain, grief, and trauma. I will close *Failure to Scream* by recording her well-articulated journey through the scream that took her to the other side and back again. Though unpublished, I always thought it should be. Now it is.

Park Avenue, Winter Park, Florida, is a street of contrasts. It is bordered on one side by a two-trains-a-day station and a tree-filled park. Spanish gray moss hangs from oak trees, where squirrels play tag up and down gnarled limbs. Sunshine filters through bright green leaves, weaving lacy patterns. Small dogs, out for their daily romp, run around frantically barking at the elusive squirrels.

Mer and I picked one of the old, worn, wooden benches and sat down where "J. K." had carved his immortality some day long ago. This is a new scene for us, I thought, as I took my long-neglected needlepoint out of the bag and tried to remember how I used to do the basket-weave stitch. I looked at my husband, who sat quietly, elbows resting on his knees, knuckles locked into each other as he stared at the ground. I look at those dear hands and remembered them the other day in the doctor's office as he reached into his pocket to pull out a shiny quarter and slid it close to the scared little red-headed boy sitting next to him on the couch. What a grin he got from his fellow conspirator as the child shyly took the offered coin.

I remembered those same hands last Christmas, skillfully carving a lump of clay in front of delighted grandchildren. First a cradle and then the baby Jesus; then presto, the cradle turned into a cross as the story of the Christ unfolded. This was the hand I had gripped hard during the long hours of the night before. "Pray for me, Ann," he whispered. "I'm sorry to keep you awake." I spoke to our heavenly Father and asked Him to take away the pain. We then sat up, propped up in bed, pillows behind us, with hands linked and sang in childlike fashion, "Praise the name of Jesus. Praise the name of Jesus. He's my rock, He's my fortress, He's my deliverer, in Him will I trust. Praise the name of Jesus." He heard our singing, and we slept through the rest of the night.

There in the park I wanted again to take his hands in mine and comfort him but knew that right now he wanted nothing more from me but the right to sort out his thoughts in his own private filing cabinet. I looked through the cars and across the street at all of the shops and storefronts we both knew so well. There people were engaged in business as usual. They darted in and out of the old-world shops and restaurants. I saw the potted daisies and azaleas in front of the florist window; the black, silk "little nothing" in the lingerie shop; and couples entering the Yum-Yum Shop, where I could smell the hamburgers cooking. People there were too occupied with their own activities even to glance across the street where we resters sat.

My thoughts played hide-and-seek with the sixteen years Mer and I had lived in Winter Park. Much of our time had been spent on Park Avenue. These were the stores and restaurants we had most frequented. Sometimes we met unplanned in the bank while cashing checks. Once he discovered me coming out of my favorite dress shop, trying to hide a new dress in the trunk of the car. Several times I came back to my parked car to find a scribbled "Mer was here" on his business card tucked into the steering wheel. Our cars gave friendly "toots" to each other as they passed. Often our brief meeting stretched into a furtive hour as we ducked into the Yum-Yum for coffee. As I admired his apricot sport coat and he approved my new hairdo, we were two different people from the Mom and Dad who ate dinner with the kids every night.

Today I looked at the still full head of silver-gray hair, which a year of chemotherapy had left untouched, and my heart wanted to encircle his pain and make it my own. How quickly, I thought, how quickly we had crossed over from the busy side of the street to the park where we now sat. Two who used to be so busy were now sitting in the park in the middle of the day. I, who had been active teaching a Bible class and speaking at Christian women's clubs, now perfectly content sitting with my husband, working needlepoint. Mer, a well-dressed salesman for Allied Van Lines a few months ago, who used to drive all over town, now confined to bed most of the time, with an occasional visit to the park or the doctor's office. How our lives had changed.

Mer absently picked at the small brown scab on the back of his hand, which never seemed to heal completely. Too many needles had fed glucose into those veins. He raised his hand, smiled at me, and said, "Time to go, Honey; I've had it. Are you ready?" "Yes, sure," I said, stuffing my needlepoint into my bag. "How's the headache?" "Well, it's still there. Just a sliver," and he raised his hand to shade his eyes from the sun. As I took his arm, I tried not to see the old polo shirt, baggy pants, and tennis shoes, which were easy for him to wear now. "Let's go back to the car, Honey." I opened the door and helped him in. As I walked around and slid into the driver's seat, I prayed he wouldn't even remember that this was the job previously relegated to him. This was our last trip to the park together. Soon Mer had to go to the hospital, where oxygen was constantly available.

One day when I was sitting by his hospital bed, needlepointing again, the phone rang. It was our daughter, calling to see how he felt. Mer surprised me by putting out his hand to take the phone from me. His weakened voice became strong and reso-nant as he said to her, "Cathy, I'm ready to be with Jesus." As the family gathered in his room late that night, my husband removed his oxygen mask, which he then used constantly, and said, "God, wait a minute; I want to talk to my family." He raised his arms up toward the ceiling and with a radiant face said to us, "Can't you hear the trumpets?" He spoke a per-sonal message to each one of us and then said, "What a beautiful day. What a beautiful family." Six hospital nurses came in and stood, some with tears streaming down their faces, all sharing with us the glory of this moment. The room seemed bathed in gold, and we were all as one person. I heard the voice of God speaking to my heart, "This is my beloved son, in whom I am well pleased," and I knew that God was going to take Mer home. A few hours later he died, and God again spoke to my heart, just two words: "He lives; he lives."

I still live a short distance from Park Avenue. Now I am walking again on the busy side of the street. As I look across through the cars, I see the still quiet park and think of the times Mer and I sat there together. I think back on that time when we lived in God's Word together, prayed and sang together, and praised God together. Now God has different things for me to do. I don't know now how long I will remain on the busy side of the street. But this one thing I do know: God lives on both sides of Park Avenue, Winter Park, Florida.[6]

God does live on both sides of the street. I believe when we fail to scream, He screams for us. When we scream, He screams along with us. He is no foreigner to either side.

NOTES

Introduction

1. *Dallas Times Herald,* 8 March 1986.

2. Ibid.

3. "22 Killed in Texas Rampage," *USA Today,* 17 October 1991.

4. "Disasters of '89 Worst in 15 Years," *USA Today,* 17 November 1989.

5. "Experts cite 10,500 deaths every year," *USA Today,* 5 September 1991.

Chapter 1

1. Charles F. Melchert, "Learning from Suffering, Silence, and Death," *The Journal of Religious Education,* 84, no. 1, 41.

2. The complete record of the Delta 191 crash has been published in the book *Fire and Rain: A Tragedy in American Aviation* (Texas Monthly Press, 1986) by Jerome Greer Chandler, who as a reporter for *Time* was at a Dallas-Fort Worth gate waiting for a flight and saw the crash. One chapter is devoted to the personnel, one of whom was the author, who cared for the families and survivors of the crash.

3. Charles R. Figley, ed., *Trauma and Its Wake: The Study and Treatment of Post-Traumatic Stress Disorder,* vol. 1 (New York: Brunner/Mazel, 1985), xviii.

4. S. Epstein, "The Self Concept Revisited," *American Psychologist,* 28 (1973), 404–16.

5. Robert Hicks, *Returning Home* (Tarrytown, N.Y.: Revell Press, 1991), 150.

6. Ronnie Janoff-Bulman, "The Aftermath of Victimization: Rebuilding Shattered Assumptions," in Figley, *Trauma and Its Wake,* 19.

7. Morton Bard and Dawn Sangrey, *The Crime Victim's Book,* 2nd ed. (New York: Brunner/Mazel), 7.

8. Ibid.

9. Hough et al., "Mental Health Consequences of Massacre," *Journal of Traumatic Stress,* 3 (1990), 86.

10. I realize that some animals may have the experience of grief and loss over one of their own kind, but it is not apparent that their lives fall apart because of the loss. Either we have something to learn from the animal kingdom, or humans are a radically different sort!

11. Bard and Sangrey, *The Crime Victim's Book,* 54.

12. Ibid., 55.

13. Viktor E. Frankl, *Man's Search for Meaning* (New York: Washington Square Press, 1984), 135.

14. Bard and Sangrey, *The Crime Victim's Book,* 62.

15. C. S. Lewis, *A Grief Observed* (London: Faber & Faber, 1961), 9.

16. Janoff-Bulman, "The Aftermath of Victimization," 23.

17. Henri J. M. Nouwen, *The Wounded Healer* (Garden City: Image Books, 1979), 37–38.

18. Ibid., 12.

19. Elie Wiesel, *Night* (New York: Bantam Books, 1960), 61–62.

20. Ibid., 32.

21. Devora Carmil and Shlomo Breznitz, "Personal Trauma and World View—Are Extremely Stressful Experiences Related to Po-

litical Attitudes, Religious Beliefs, and Future Orientation?" *Journal of Traumatic Stress,* 4 (1991), 393–405.

22. Janoff-Bulman, "The Aftermath of Victimization," 22.

23. Benyakar et al., "The Collapse of a Structure: A Structural Approach to Trauma," *Journal of Traumatic Stress,* 2 (1989), 437.

24. Ibid., 442.

Chapter 2

1. C. S. Lewis, "Relapse," *Poems,* ed. Walter Hooper (New York: Harcourt Brace Jovanovich, 1964), 103–4.

2. William Shakespeare, *Hamlet,* act 3, sc. 1, lines 57–60.

3. Charles R. Figley and Hamilton I. McCubbin, eds., "Catastrophes: an Overview of Family Reactions," *Stress and the Family,* vol. 2 (New York: Brunner/ Mazel, 1983), 10.

4. "Tribute to Ramstein disaster 'saints,'" *The Stars and Stripes,* 11 August 1989, 10.

5. *Diagnostic and Statistical Manual of Mental Disorders,* 3rd ed. (Washington, D.C.: American Psychiatric Association, 1985), 236.

6. Ibid.

7. Bartone and Wright, "Grief and Group Recovery Following a Military Air Disaster," *Journal of Traumatic Stress,* 3 (1990), 528–29.

8. Story written and told to the author by Robert J. Friske about his father, Edward J. Friske, World War II veteran, 6 October 1991. Used by permission.

9. Sonia Moore writes about this method in *The Stanislavsky System* (New York: Penguin Books, 1984), 42–43: "The actor is capable of stirring a needed emotion within himself only because he has often experienced analogous emotion in his own life. Every experience in life leaves a trace on our central nervous system, and thus the nerves which participate in a given experience become more sensitive to such a stimulus. . . . The emotional memory not

only retains an imprint of an experience but also synthesizes feelings of a different nature."

10. *Diagnostic and Statistical Manual,* 236.

11. Heard in a small-group session, Society for Traumatic-Stress Studies conference, Baltimore, 1987.

12. Study done with the cooperation of 550 colleagues working in the field of traumatic stress. Published by Rosalyn Schultz, Bennett Braun, and Richard Kluft, Department of Psychiatry and Human Behavior, Saint Louis University Medical Center, August 1987.

13. T. H. Holmes and M. Masuda, "Life Change and Illness Susceptibility," in *Stressful Life Events,* ed. Barbara and Bruce Dohrenwend (New York: Wiley, 1974), 42–72.

14. Bard and Sangrey, *The Crime Victim's Book,* 20.

15. Ibid., 19.

16. Kilpatrick, Veronen, and Best, "Factors Predicting Psychological Distress Among Rape Victims," in Figley, *Trauma and Its Wake,* 117.

17. Hicks, *Returning Home,* 99.

18. *Diagnostic and Statistical Manual,* 238.

19. These conclusions are included in a paper the author produced for the course Critical-Incident Stress, taught at Maxwell Air Force Base Chaplains' School, Montgomery, Alabama. Briefing materials are titled *Research on Trauma Ministry* by Maj. Robert M. Hicks, Pennsylvania Air National Guard, 1988.

20. Elisabeth Kubler-Ross, "Afraid to Die," *Pastoral Psychology,* June 1972, 41–51.

21. Carl A. Nighswonger, "Ministry to the Dying as a Learning Encounter," *The Journal of Pastoral Care,* 26 (1972), 41–51.

22. I do not believe that Job was given this disease because he was self-righteous. Job never knew why he had the disease and rightly wrestled with God over the injustice of it. Job provides the modern reader a relevant and valuable portrait of the innocent sufferer who bargains and argues with God over his trauma.

23. Therese A. Rando, *Grief, Dying, and Death* (Champaign, Ill.: Research Press, 1984), 28–29.

24. Kathleen Gilbert, as quoted by Robert Hicks, "How to Survive the Loss of a Child," *Husbands and Wives* (Wheaton: Victor Books, 1988), 434.

25. Figley, *Trauma and Its Wake,* 403.

Chapter 3

1. Nouwen, *The Wounded Healer,* xvi.

2. Figley and McCubbin, *Stress and the Family,* 159.

3. William Shakespeare, *Macbeth,* act 4, sc. 3, lines 209–10.

4. Bard and Sangrey, *The Crime Victim's Book,* 69.

5. The situation is unjust because both the woman and the man, by Jewish law, were to be stoned for adultery (Deut. 22:22). The scene is thus set up to trap Jesus. For the woman, despite her reasons for being where she was, it was an injustice on the part of the religious leaders. Jesus did not overlook the fact of her sin but merely pointed out that the only one capable of real judgment is the one who is sinless. The sin of the woman was then expanded to all standing there, except, of course, Jesus, who was sinless. He said, "Neither do I condemn you" (v. 11), confirming God's view of even a sinner.

6. Press information for the video *A Quiet Hope,* Bridgestone Group, Carlsbad, Calif., 1991.

7. Sandra K. Burge, "Rape: Individual and Family Reactions," in Figley and McCubbin, *Stress and the Family,* 112.

8. Figley and McCubbin, *Stress and the Family,* 31.

9. Yael Danieli, "The Treatment and Prevention of Long-term Effects and Intergenerational Transmission of Victimization: A Lesson from Holocaust Survivors and Their Children," in Figley, *Trauma and Its Wake,* 301–2.

10. John F. Crosby and Nancy L. Jose, "Death: Family Adjustment to Loss," in Figley and McCubbin, *Stress and the Family,* 81–82.

11. Patricia Voydanoff, "Unemployment: Family Strategies for Adaptation," in Figley and McCubbin, *Stress and the Family,* 90–91.

12. Deborah Tannen, *You Just Don't Understand* (New York: Ballantine Books, 1990), 24–25.

Chapter 4

1. William Shakespeare, *As You Like It,* act 2, sc. 1, lines 12–14.

2. C. S. Lewis, *The Problem of Pain* (New York: Macmillan, 1962), 157.

3. Julius Segal, *Winning Life's Toughest Battles* (New York: McGraw-Hill, 1986), xii.

4. Ibid., 2–3, 9.

5. Marsha Tansey Four, "We Were the Invisible Force," *The Philadelphia Inquirer,* 11 November 1991.

6. Briefing by the United States Navy Sprint Team (Rapid Intervention Team) on the role of the navy Seals in the Air Florida crash, the Association of Military Surgeon Generals Conference, Las Vegas, 10 November 1987.

7. Eugene B. McDaniel, *Scars and Stripes* (reprint, Philadelphia: A. J. Holman, 1975), 101.

8. C. S. Lewis, *The Problem of Pain,* 116.

9. In the military, levels of care are categorized by: first eschelon, which is buddy care, for example, a buddy's stopping his friend's bleeding; second, a field-hospital collection point, with trained medical personnel and surgery unit (MASH); and third, a full-range medical facility. In the Vietnam War most psychological and spiritual personnel were concentrated in the third eschelon. This level is now considered too late in the intervention process. Chaplains and mental-health professionals need to be on the front lines.

10. Also noted by Jeffrey Mitchell, "Acute Stress Reactions: Military Perspectives and Suggested Intervention Strategies," 82.

11. Herbert Hendin and Ann Pollinger Haas, *Wounds of War: the Psychological Aftermath of Combat in Vietnam* (New York: Basic Books, 1984), 221.

12. J. J. Card, "Epidemiology of PTSD in a national cohort of Vietnam veterans," *Journal of Clinical Psychology,* 43 (1987), 6–17.

13. Cited in Segal, *Winning Life's Toughest Battles,* 18.

14. Study done at one-week, six-week, and six-month intervals on ninety-six people who suffered major flood damage in Roanoke, Va. The mere perception and knowledge that financial assistance and social-agency support were available were critical in lowering initial traumatic symptoms. Jerome D. Cook and Leonard Bickman, "Social Support and Psychological Symptomatology Following a Natural Disaster," *Journal of Traumatic Stress,* 3 (1990), 541–56.

15. Story told by General Dozier at the Armed Forces Communications and Electronic Association banquet, Philadelphia.

16. Story told by FBI agent who worked with the Iran hostage crisis, Society for Traumatic-Stress Studies conference, Baltimore, 1987.

17. Quoted in Segal, *Winning Life's Toughest Battles,* 35.

18. Rando, *Grief, Dying, and Death,* 402–3.

19. Vanderlyn R. Pine and Carolyn Brauer, "Parental Grief: a Synthesis of Theory, Research, and Intervention," *Parental Loss of a Child,* ed. Therese A. Rando (Champaign, Ill.: Research Press, 1986), 73.

20. Hendin and Haas, *Wounds of War,* 47–48.

21. Robert Hicks, in Phillip Yancey, *Disappointment with God* (Grand Rapids: Zondervan, 1988), 254–55.

22. Quoted in Segal, *Winning Life's Toughest Battles,* 57.

23. Ibid., 71–72.

24. After-action report by Chaplain 1st Lt. Gregory Clapper, Iowa Air National Guard, 186th Tactical Fighter Group, Sioux City Gateway Airport, 19 July 1989.

25. Burge, "Rape: Individual and Family Reactions," 109.

26. Segal, *Winning Life's Toughest Battles,* 87.

27. Unpublished research by Col. Robert Ursano and Carol Fullerton, Uniformed Services University of the Health Sciences,

Bethesda, Maryland. Research presented at the Air Force Chaplains' School, October 1990, and in private conversations with Dr. Fullerton.

28. Clapper, after-action report, 4.

Chapter 5

1. Dusty, "I Went to Vietnam to Heal," in *Visions of War, Dreams of Peace,* ed. Lynda Van Devanter and Joan A. Furey (New York: Warner Books, 1991), 117.

2. William Sloane Coffin, "My Son Beat Me to the Grave," *Christian Home,* fall 1985, 22.

3. William Blake, "On Another's Sorrow," *The Essential Blake,* ed. Stanley Kunitz (New York: Ecco Press, 1987), 24.

4. Frankl, *Man's Search for Meaning,* 141.

5. Ibid., 97.

6. Yancey, *Disappointment with God,* 253.

7. See Stanton L. Jones and Richard E. Butman, *Modern Psychotherapies* (Downers Grove: InterVarsity, 1991), 85–88, for an excellent overview of this era's assumptions.

8. M. Scott Peck, *People of the Lie* (New York: Simon and Schuster, 1983), 10.

9. John Steinbeck, *The Grapes of Wrath* (New York: Viking, 1939), 32.

10. Routledge and Kegan Paul, eds., John Stuart Mill, *Essays of Ethics, Religion, and Society,* vol. 10 of *The Collected Works of John Stuart Mill* (Toronto: University of Toronto, 1969), 385.

11. Hendin and Haas, *Wounds of War,* 213.

12. Charles R. Figley, ed., *Stress Disorders among Vietnam Veterans* (New York: Brunner/Mazel, 1978), 149–50.

13. Chaim F. Shatan, "Stress Disorders Among Vietnam Veterans: the Emotional Context of Combat Continues," in Figley, *Stress Disorders,* 48.

14. Paul Ramsey, *War and the Christian Conscience* (Durham: Duke University, 1961), 115.

15. *What Everyone Should Know About Jewish Holidays, Festivals, and Fast Days* (Greenfield, Mass.: Channing L. Bete, 1979), 7.

16. I have used the word *begins* at this point because I believe that forgiveness is also a process. Just because God forgives does not mean that suddenly and magically all psychological traces of our guilt and remorse are removed. I will say more about this in chapter 6.

17. Christopher Lasch, *The Culture of Narcissism* (New York: Warner Books, 1979), 33, 103.

18. One cannot really conceive or prove a best-of-all-possible-worlds concept. Whatever world we might conceive, the moment we define it, we make it possible to conceive a better one. If the best of all possible worlds is a fast car, girls, steaks, and ice cream, then the moment I conceive it, someone can imagine a better world with faster cars, more or better-looking girls, better steaks, and more ice cream. Thus, the best of all possible worlds is impossible to conceive or prove. See Alvin C. Plantinga's excellent treatment of the argument in *God, Freedom, and Evil* (Grand Rapids: Eerdmans, 1974).

19. *A Quiet Hope,* documentary video.

20. Frankl, *Man's Search for Meaning,* 162.

21. *The Cost of Discipleship* by Bonhoeffer details the meaning of this hope to this pastor who gave his life opposing the Nazi regime.

22. "Slain Hostage's Body Brought Back to U.S.," *The Charlotte Observer,* 25 December 1991.

23. Personal letter to the author by an administrative supervisor of a Dallas hospital that treated crash victims, 1 May 1988.

24. Rick Peterson and La Vone Sopher, "Plane Crash," *American Journal of Nursing,* October 1989, 1288–89.

25. Clapper, after-action report, 3.

26. Colonel Maloney has been the chief of Medical Examination Services at Dover Air Force Base and has personally supervised and staffed the Gander U.S. Army Airborne air crash, the Challenger space-shuttle explosion, and the U.S. Marine Corps barracks terrorist attack in Lebanon. He probably knows more about this field than anyone in America. The writer has served on various panels with him and has shared podiums at the previously mentioned surgeon general's conference, the Society for Traumatic-Stress Studies conferences, and the USAF Chaplains' School's Critical-Incident Stress course.

27. In one of Jeff Mitchell's training films he interviews a policeman who had to carry out the body of a baby whose head had been severed by his insane father. The policeman, needless to say, had developed a serious case of posttraumatic-stress disorder, which caused many continuing problems.

Chapter 6

1. Ernest Hemingway, *A Farewell to Arms,* as quoted in William Sloane Coffin, "My Son Beat Me to the Grave," 22.

2. Marilyn McMahon, "Wounds of War," in Van Devanter and Furey, *Visions of War,* 87.

3. Henry Brandt, *When You're Tired of Treating the Symptoms, and You're Ready for a Cure, Give Me a Call* (Brentwood, Tenn.: Wolgemuth & Hyatt, 1991), 131–32.

4. "When Can Memories Be Trusted?" *Time,* 28 Oct. 1991, 86–88.

5. Richard Restak, *The Brain* (New York: Bantam Books, 1984), 174.

6. Ibid., 212–14.

7. Bernie Zilbergeld, *The Shrinking of America: the Myth of Psychological Change* (Boston: Little, Brown, 1983), 1.

8. Ibid., 265, 267.

9. Larry Crabb, a Christian psychologist, is a good example of one

who uses this method but also substitutes something for the naked vulnerability. See *Inside Out* by Dr. Crabb.

10. John White, *Changing on the Inside* (Ann Arbor: Servant Publications, 1991), 52.

11. For the history of the concept see Charles L. Whitfield, *Healing the Child Within* (Pompano Beach, Fla.: Health Communications, 1987), 5–8.

12. Ibid., 9.

13. See Earl D. Wilson, *The Undivided Self* (Downers Grove: InterVarsity, 1983), 11.

14. John Bradshaw, *Healing the Shame That Binds You* (Deerfield Beach, Fla.: Health Communications, 1988), 171.

15. Ibid., 172. Also see his *Homecoming, Reclaiming and Championing Your Inner Child,* 207, 1160, in which he suggests both talking and writing letters to the inner child.

16. Several counselors have observed that generally, women are helped more by this than men are. Men focus more on concrete aspects of their pain, and as externally engaging the world, they may need more action-oriented means to bring about this inner healing.

17. I have much appreciation for Bradshaw's ability in diagnosis and articulation. His packaging of some difficult concepts is excellent. However, since his theory is still personally driven by his own experience, as all theories are, it is my opinion that he is still reacting to his harsh religious upbringing. Consequently, his theory has little room for true moral guilt (as opposed to psychological shame) or the concept of universal right and wrong. It seems that he has a serious ax to grind against the church, God (in traditional terms), and institutional religion. See *Homecoming, Reclaiming and Championing Your Inner Child,* 272–76, for his personal story of hurt by his Basilian order and study in a Catholic seminary.

18. David A. Seamands, *Healing of Memories* (Wheaton: Victor Books, 1985), 140.

19. Daryl E. Quick, *The Healing Journey for Adult Children of Alcoholics* (Downers Grove: InterVarsity, 1990), 121.

20. Dennis Linn and Matthew Linn, *Healing Life's Hurts* (New York: Paulist Press, 1978), 2.

21. Leanne Payne, *The Healing Presence* (Westchester, Ill.: Crossway Books, 1989), 31.

22. Leanne Payne, *The Broken Image* (Westchester, Ill.: Crossway Books, 1981), 146.

23. Payne, *The Healing Presence*, 192.

24. Don't take this statement in the typical American application of Aristotelian thinking. The human-potential movement has convinced us that we must have a peak performance in every area of life. What a guilt trip that lays on us average, mediocre humans. For me to experience one new emotion was worth the trip through mid-life (I think!).

25. Eugene H. Peterson, "Growth: an Act of the Will?" *Leadership*, 9, no. 4, 34–40, as cited in John White, *Changing on the Inside*, 89–90.

26. Eugene Van Ness Goethius, *The Language of the New Testament* (New York: Scribner's Sons, 1965), 104.

27. John R. Stott, *The Cross of Christ* (Downers Grove: InterVarsity, 1986), 331.

28. Ibid., 332.

29. The author's contemporary paraphrase of the story Jesus told in Luke 15:11–32.

30. John White, *Changing on the Inside*, 115.

31. Ibid., 50.

32. Lewis B. Smedes, *Forgive and Forget* (New York: Simon and Schuster, 1984), 126.

33. Colin Brown, ed., *Dictionary of New Testament Theology*, vol. 1, s.v. "Forgiveness" (Grand Rapids: Zondervan, 1975), 697–703.

34. Leanne Payne, *The Healing Presence*, 33.

35. Adapted from Smedes, *Forgive and Forget,* 126–57.

36. Ibid., 83.

37. Ibid., 89.

38. In New Testament Greek the words *joy* and *grace* share the same root, *char. Joy* is *chara,* while *grace* is *charis.* See Brown, *Dictionary of New Testament Theology,* vol. 2, 115.

39. Jill Smolowe, "Lives in Limbo: the Ordeal," *Time,* 16 Dec. 1991, 20.

40. Mary Beyers Garrison, "Recovery," in Van Devanter and Furey, *Visions of War,* 63.

41. See Rando, *Grief, Dying, and Death,* 104–8, on the role of rituals in grief.

42. Ibid., 104.

43. Ibid., 105–6.

44. At this point I do not want to discuss the long-standing theological differences regarding the exact nature and meaning of the ceremony. Catholics call it a sacrament that imparts grace because the bread and the wine become the actual flesh and blood of Jesus. Protestants generally have either seen the ceremony as a mere remembrance or memorial of what Jesus did or have believed that Jesus is present in some way that is different from the real presence in which Catholics believe.

45. Linn and Linn, *Healing Life's Hurts,* 185–86.

46. Raymond M. Scurfield, "Post-trauma Stress: Assessment and Treatment: Overview and Formulations," in Figley, *Trauma and Its Wake,* 241–50.

47. Ibid., 250.

Conclusion

1. Paul Bartone, "Person, Environments, and the Management of Stress," paper presented at the Eleventh Biennial Symposium on Psychology, Department of Defense, Colorado Springs, April 1988, 1–5.

2. Ibid., 2.

3. Emda Orr and Mina Westman, "Hardiness as a Stress Moderator: Literature Review," study presented at the Fourth International Conference on Psychological Stress in Times of War and Peace, Tel Aviv, 8–12 January 1989, program abstracts, 50.

4. Story told to the author by Bobbie Trotter, American Red Cross nurse, South Vietnam, 1970–71.

5. Bobbie Trotter, "I Know You've Waited," in Van Devanter and Furey, *Visions of War,* 48.

6. Mer's death was both a tragedy and a triumph. I officiated at his funeral and saw the overwhelming impact of his life on nurses, business associates, people he had moved as part of his job, and even his barber. He was a man who enjoyed life, his family, and his God. His well-known generosity was personally enjoyed by this author, who valued being his son-in-law. Ann Rosenburg continues to walk on both sides of the street, a source of wisdom and love to her children; her grandchildren; and to me, her son-in-law.